Write
Pray
Recover

A Journey to Wellness Through Spiritual Solutions and Self Care

by Wendy I. Blanchard
M.S., INHC, NYCPS

Testimonials

"With grace, love, and authentic voice, Wendy Blanchard not only brings you through her (on-going) process of Recovery, but offers accessible solutions and practical tools for ours. She moves beyond traditional "talk therapy" and mutual aid to an emphasis on self-care, somatic, holistic methods and deepening a connection to spirit. WRITE PRAY RECOVER is a must read for people in recovery, family members in recovery, and health care practitioners, as a guide to helping ourselves as we help others."

Theresa M. Knorr, CARC
BALANCE Recovery Consultation | Tai Chi for Recovery
Director of Education and Training, Friends of Recovery – New York

"I have witnessed in amazement at the courage, stamina and determination that Wendy Blanchard has demonstrated in her journey to recovery. She is an outstanding role model for anyone struggling with addiction and has utilized everything that she has learned about addiction to aid in her recovery. It has been a heartwarming journey that will inspire those who read her book".

Mignyetta C. Ramnani, LCSWR
Within Reach Counseling Services

"Vulnerability and strength. Steel wrapped in Cotton. Thoughts of the person who I know as Wendy Blanchard. Wendy looks beyond the traditional 12-step recovery program by recognizing that abstinence and relationship with a Higher Power would provide a part of her recovery journey. This courageous and self-aware survivor reaches to the core of her being with a willingness to change everything about herself. Most importantly, she shares her journey openly with grace and respect for the tremendous effort required to adjust one's narrative. Her message illustrates opportunity in each "Now Moment" as opportunity for growth. I know she is a miracle worker."

Brian Bailey, Lieutenant Colonel, United States Army, Retired

"Thank you so much for last night's program. It was raw and downright emotional. Sharing your story lets others hear how painful it is to have a loved one with mental health issues and promotes an open dialogue on mental health. Through your professional intuition and guidance, I believe this program was one of the most important workshops our library has ever had."

Lynne Warshavsky
Event Coordinator
Orangeburg Library

This is THAT book you want to highlight, keep close for daily reference and buy one for everyone you love! Wendy's inspiring vulnerability, honesty, insightful and intuitive tools I will apply personally and proudly share with my clients. *Write, Pray, Recover* isn't just a book you read, it's one that changes your life through powerful stories, connection to spirit and your healthiest truest self. It's a book you devour and live!

Jill Anenberg Lawrence
Holistic Nutritionist, Health Coach

 FriesenPress

One Printers Way
Altona, MB R0G 0B0
Canada

www.friesenpress.com

ISBN
978-1-03-912661-9 (Hardcover)
978-1-03-912660-2 (Paperback)
978-1-03-912662-6 (eBook)

1. *Self-Help, Substance Abuse & Addictions*

Distributed to the trade by The Ingram Book Company

"Self-Care Is The Actions That We Take To Achieve Wellness, And Wellness Is Where We Stand In Our Power!"

— Wendy Blanchard, M.S., INHC, NYCPS

For my loving children,
Matthew, Nicole, and Olivia,
my soul daughter, Sarah,
and my granddaughter, Rose Olivia,
for inspiring me to live.

For my granddaughter, Harper Sydney,
for enhancing my life, and that of our family.

Foreword

I've known Wendy since early 2018. Not long you may say, but it feels a lot longer. Wendy at that time was going through a difficult period in her personal life, yet seemed to have this mental resilience, which I found admirable. What I soon discovered was a lady who has a strong sense of identity combined with a wonderful set of core values. In life there are two types of people, I believe: those who strive to survive and those who strive to thrive. Wendy is most definitely residing in the latter. Even though Wendy is now in her early sixties, to me it feels like observing a much younger woman embarking on a mission. Her energy, drive, and determination put many others in the shade, as she goes about her daily activities squeezing the juice out of this opportunity we call life.

Over the last nine months or so, I have had the pleasure of mentoring Wendy on certain aspects of mindset growth, as well as social media and sharing her message with the world. Wendy embraced the challenges that I set for her with enthusiasm and without complaint. We began to deliver live Facebook videos on health and mindset to a global audience. Even though secretly I'm sure Wendy was nervous before the live broadcasts, she was actually riveting to watch, explaining her ideas, imparting great information to the viewing audience on subjects such as nutrition, resilience, meditation, and exercise. This was delivered with passion, integrity, and with the hope that, if it helped even one person watching, then it would have been a job well done.

One of the great qualities of Wendy Blanchard I have noticed with her clients, workshops, and work in the community is that she is very giving. There is an immense sense that she gives without asking, gives without expectation, and gives without fear. I'm sure you'll agree that these qualities are very rare in this modern day.

Yet behind this life of service and excellence lies a story of excruciating pain and an unenviable history of mental, emotional and physical abuse. I believe that, in life, some people will succumb to the pain and remain as victims, or as in Wendy's case, go on to use the experience as a platform to help others escape their pain. We live our life by choices and decisions made in the moment. Moments that define us. Moments that can make or break us. Moments that change our destiny forever. In reading this book, you will learn the story (the way) and the tools, techniques, and strategies (the how) that Wendy uses to assist so many people to live better lives.

It's not uncommon to hear stories of Wendy answering distress calls, immediately going to the aid of potential suicide victims, and rescuing and supporting them in their darkest hour. For me, this book will facilitate a profound difference in people's lives globally, and offer hope to those who believe that they are not good enough or not worthy enough, and feel that they are on the scrap heap of life. This book offers solutions through lived experience.

By utilizing the knowledge within this book, Wendy will be able to assist you from its pages and offer you guidance, and the wisdom that she has accrued from her journey into hell and back. The words contained within this tome are the words of someone who refuses to give up, who believes in patience and persistence, and who would dearly love for you to experience self-love and self-respect through the eyes of self-care and Spirituality.

Self-care will require you, the reader, to exercise both consistent daily practice and relentless focus. As you practice the tools Wendy shares with you, and focus on becoming the best version of you, life will suddenly feel that much more joyous.

David Rahman
Mind Coach & International Speaker
May 23rd 2019

"Practice gratitude, and experience extraordinary joy in all of the ordinary moments."

– Wendy Blanchard, M.S., INHC, NYCPS

Introduction

E arly on the morning of April 3, 2013, I knew that if I did not get help to treat my addiction to prescription drugs, and my mental illness, I was going to die. As if speaking directly to me, the morning news anchor looked directly into the camera, explained that prescription drug addiction was on the rise, and said the words, "You can get help. You are not alone."

In the next few weeks, after a lifetime of struggles, an angel visited me and restored my hope through the beautiful, kind, and loving souls that walk with me. I felt a bit lost, albeit still firm in my faith, and I needed reassurance of a powerful magnitude. The Universe/God/Spirit sent an earthquake of love that shook me to my deepest core. I walked away with some bumps and bruises but filled with renewed faith, hope, trust, and love. My foundation was still intact, and I was given the opportunity to rebuild my life.

After a lifetime of living with substance use disorder and multi occurring mental health disorders, I experienced a spiritual awakening. I experienced a "knowing" that if I did not speak my truth and ask for help immediately, my death would be imminent. I could literally feel a Divine presence surrounding me. Supporting me. Guiding me. Within me, I felt a peace I had never before encountered. I heard an inner voice say, "It's time to call for help. Everything will be alright."

As I reflect on both challenges and blessings, I am so grateful for this journey. Through faith, hope, and love, I continue to thrive in my recovery in wellness—body, mind, and spirit. I have had the opportunity to learn so much about myself: my determination, my resilience, my strengths, and where I need to continue to build. I've discovered the depth of love that I feel for my family and loved ones, my passion, and my strong faith, which is the foundation of my wellness. I've learned so much about life and about all of us who have our daily challenges. I have observed how we all do our best to rise above adversity. I am encouraged by the interconnectedness of the human spirit. I am further encouraged, and humbled by God/Spirit/Universe's loving guidance which is at the foundation of my wellness. I opened my heart to love, and opened my mind to new perspectives, and instantly felt loved and supported. We are never alone. This, my beautiful souls, is the power of love.

I decided from the moment that I came out of the rehabilitation facility, in 2013, that I was going to write a book about my lifelong prescription-drug addiction. I want to help to raise awareness and eliminate the stigma of this chronic and progressive brain disease, in an effort to save lives. I had been unwell for forty years, and never told anyone due to the fear and shame that addiction and mental health disorders brought along with them. My purpose is to help normalize these disorders by sparking a dialogue and letting it filter worldwide.

In addition, I immediately realized that I would need to create a completely new way of living, and I had heard so much about living a holistic lifestyle that the idea enveloped me. Immediately upon discharge from the rehabilitation facility, I began researching and exploring natural and organic solutions, foods, spirituality, and everything I could find, on holistic living. Subsequently, I decided to go back to school to earn my certification in holistic health counseling, and my book took on a whole new trajectory. I created my "Wellness Approach to Recovery."

In addition to earning a certification in holistic health counseling, I earned my certification as a Peer Specialist from the Office of Mental Health NYS. I earned certifications in many areas of mental health and Substance Use Disorder, including "Suicide Safety for Schools," "Mental Health First Aid," "De-Escalation," "Trauma Informed Care," "Motivational Interviewing," "Spiritual Wellness," "SafeTalk," "How to Implement Social and Emotional Learning using Conflict Resolution and Restorative Practices-A CRC Model," "SEL as a Lever for Equity and Social Justice," "Emotional Literacy," "Mental Health Education Law," "NARCAN," "CPR," and "MAT," just to name a few.

I went on to create my much sought after workshop training, entitled, "Mental Health and Wellness Literacy," another entitled, "Whole Person Wellness – The Gut/Brain Axis," and a series of three workshop trainings entitled "Whole Person Wellness: Reset Your Mindset, Reignite Your Health, Recharge Your Life!" One of the workshops is for the general public, one is for school staff, and one is for those in recovery or living with substance use disorder and/or mental health disorders. This third workshop is called Whole Person Wellness: An Integrative Approach to Recovery. All are in great demand within our community!

In my private practice, I work with clients who are seeking to implement sustainable lifestyle changes through natural and organic solutions using an integrative approach. If the client chooses to use both recovery models of a holistic approach and a traditional medical approach simultaneously, I work as a part of the treatment team.

I created this book so that those living with substance use disorder and mental health disorders will know that this is a brain disease that is diagnosable, treatable, and manageable, and that you are not alone. In addition, I offer specific guidance to the wellness-based practices of my "Wellness Approach to Recovery" program. This is all about "my journey to wellness through spiritual solutions and self-care."

Each chapter offers personal stories, from my active addiction and recovery, and the tools that I use to move back towards wellness. I have also added in many quotes that I have written throughout the years of my recovery, each one strategically chosen to align with the chapter stories and wellness strategies. Lastly, at the end of each chapter, you will find self-reflection questions and plenty of space to write about how my stories and/or quotes resonate with you, as well as your own existing wellness/self-care practices.

If you prefer not to write in this book, grab an empty notebook as a journal, or use Google Docs, or whatever best serves you in reflective and expressive writing.

The very end of the book provides daily reflection questions, which I suggest you use to memorialize all of *your* experiences. This will be your guide as you navigate throughout your recovery—especially for the first few years.

"I am a survivor. I am not my past defined by a disease that temporarily altered my being. I am a warrior who now holds the space for others to experience their authentic selves in the present moment. This is a blessing and a gift. I am here as a vessel to usher the boat away from the shore. The waves do not hold me back as I have learned to navigate, and swim right into the waves. I've learned to go with the flow, and to feel the sun lighting my way on my journey. I live with great pride, and in peace, as I continue to experience the ripples and waves in un-chartered territory. I continue to evolve, poised for the next rush of waves, with certainty of my strength, always grateful for new opportunities to grow. I am a survivor."

– Wendy Blanchard, M.S., INHC, NYCPS

CHAPTER 1
"Look Up Child"

"Look up child; look up…"
- sung by Lauren Daigle

O penly and honestly admitting my addiction to prescription pills was the most frightening step that I ever decided to take in my life … and the most courageous. I realized that once I spoke my truth, there would be no turning back to that lifestyle. The apprehension of what others were going to say and the uncertainty of living a sober life without my "crutches," caused me a tremendous amount of anxiety—ten times as much as that which had consumed me every day since I was a very young child. I agonized for years, trying to stop numbing my emotional and physical pain to no avail. I agonized until it was crystal clear to me that, if I did not make an immediate change, my death would be imminent. In early 2013, I awoke from an overdose of prescription pills after being completely unconscious for two days. The day had come. I heard God/Spirit/Universe (whichever noun resonates with you) say, "Call for help. Everything will be alright." I have been listening to that voice ever since.

Look up child…

I began abusing prescription drugs at age fourteen to numb my physical pain from endometriosis. Upon taking my first pill, I realized that the calm, "high" feeling (the same feeling you get when you feel "buzzed" from alcohol) was exactly the way I wanted to feel in order to numb the ongoing trauma I was experiencing at home. For many, "home" is a haven of support and comfort, but in our "home," dysfunction, abuse, neglect, rage, anger, depression, anxiety, and disease were present. It smothered me in most every moment that I inhaled, making it hard for me to breathe. At fourteen, I was cutting my wrists as a form of non-suicidal self-harm and had developed an eating disorder. These behaviors were filling a void, helping me to believe the illusion that I could manage the chaos and fear that stalked me from the time I woke up until I went to sleep. It was also a cry for help, but nobody heard me. I lived in a constant state of fight, flight, or freeze, equipped with zero coping skills. Domestic abuse stole my peace, as did the excessive physical and emotional absence of my father. Sadly, both of my parents lived with their own mental health and substance use disorders. My parents coped with prescription drugs, alcohol, and destructive behaviors: hence, my own learned behavior. We absolutely "live what we learn." We also know that mental illness and substance use disorder are genetic, and that environment is a contributing factor. I was doomed to repeat these behaviors.

Unfortunately, not only did I witness domestic abuse, I suffered sexual abuse at the age of fourteen. An ex-boyfriend, who was eighteen and had already been in jail once, and five of his friends molested me as I was walking to the local movie theater where my then current boyfriend was working. On a cold February afternoon, they surrounded me on a busy highway. These young "men" put their hands inside of my bra, and in my underwear, laughing and shouting obscenities the entire time. I screamed and tried to push them off of me, to no avail. I can remember feeling a dizzy heaviness in my head as I sat there on the cold ground, stunned, while they walked away laughing. Cars whizzed by as I stood up, straightened out my clothes, brushed myself off, and continued my walk.

I arrived at the theatre, smiled, and sat down to watch the movie, and never told anyone what had happened to me that day. I now know that the trauma which I experienced, and that which I never processed, profoundly affected my mental health. As I learned many years later, our mental health is directly related to our physical health. I would spend the next forty years struggling with my health (mental, physical, and spiritual) and substance use disorder, all in an unhealthy attempt to numb the memories, the noise in my head, the abuse, the neglect, the dysfunction, the rage, the screaming, the threats ... all of it. I lived in the midst of a Tsunami and clung to the closest thing that I could to survive: a prescription for Codeine Sulfate. It saved me, temporarily.

With all of these stressors, it is unsurprising that I lived in constant terror, and this stress took a toll on my body. I always felt unwell. My severe anxiety sometimes caused me to have an uncontrolled bowel movement without warning, wherever I was. The gut/brain connection is real. We know that our gut and brain are directly connected, and when we are stressed, we can experience many forms of gastrointestinal stress. These problems continued into my adulthood and manifested in a form of inflammatory bowel disease (IBD), specifically ulcerative colitis, known to be exacerbated by stress. We know that IBD causes long-lasting inflammation and ulcers (sores) in your digestive tract, and it causes rectal bleeding. Subsequently, I was diagnosed with irritable bowel syndrome (IBS), which is also exacerbated by stress. It is characterized by a group of symptoms that occur together, including repeated pain in the abdomen and extreme changes in bowel movements.

I did receive some counseling short-term, but I never truly unearthed all of the dirt piled up in my cellular structure, planted there by the severe trauma. We know that, when we suffer trauma, it seeps into our cellular structure. The energy of the trauma is stored in our bodies' tissues until it can be released. We must be able to identify it by acknowledging it, and giving it a voice so that it can begin to move out of our body. I was never given the opportunity to release it. My brain disconnected from the reality of the trauma for self-protection, and I self-medicated for four decades to stay in a constant state of euphoria and inebriation to avoid the memories. Because of this, I could not do the work needed to relive the trauma—to work through it, accept it, and release it. I was always terrified to talk about the traumatic events with anyone, because I feared a complete mental breakdown and felt that I would never recover. I never felt safe.

The accumulated effects of my emotional "un-wellness" took a devastating toll on my health. My body had declined to such a poor state that even before I asked for help, I suffered many health issues in addition to IBD and IBS, such as lupus, a painful disease which systemically affects the joints and muscles, organs (kidneys and lungs) that no longer functioned normally because of my drug use, neurotransmitters in my brain that were all but deadened from the toxicity of the pills, and a general lack of nourishment. I was diagnosed with a rare blood disorder called MGUS, which required oncology/hematology treatments for nine years. In addition, my laryngopharyngeal reflux (LPR) severely affected my ability to digest, causing me to spit up and/or vomit up any food or even water that I attempted to swallow. I also had systemic candida, which is an overgrowth of yeast that affects the brain and organs, making them unable to function properly. The candida/yeast was causing complications systemically, and affecting both my physical and mental health.

These symptoms were being severely exacerbated by the drugs that I was ingesting daily. In addition to the other conditions, I experienced mental issues commonly associated with drug use. Confused and disoriented, I struggled to complete my thoughts because I would fall asleep mid-sentence. I slept all day, and stayed awake all night. I suffered from a drug-induced paranoid psychosis where I believed I was being watched in my home through the heating vents, the television, and my stereo speakers. Even driving short distances, I would experience severe lightheadedness and fainting spells, where I was able to stay awake just long enough to pull over and call 911.

I lived with suicidal thoughts/behaviors and self-harming behaviors. Due to the severity of my self-harm, I wound up in the hospital for emergency. surgery for a partial hysterectomy at age forty-two.

I intentionally caused myself to bleed by abusing birth-control pills. I wanted attention. I wanted to be "loved." I believed that if I were gravely ill, I would be loved. I kept all of the trauma pushed way down, and when it began to rise up, I exercised "control" with the only coping skills that I had. Drugs. Self harm. Suicidal behaviors. Addictions.

All of these problems became so critical that in 2006, I was told by one of my doctors, "There is nothing more that we can do to help you." They told me to prepare my family for my inevitable passing. Neither my primary-care physician nor my specialists had any idea that it was my addiction causing my grave health status. Not until after I began my recovery did my doctors tell me that they had suspected my addiction, and one did say, "You had us all fooled." Not one of them could figure out what was causing me to be so gravely ill.

In addition, in 2003, I took a serious fall down a flight of stairs and suffered a torn rotator cuff, which deepened the need for more painkillers. Secretly, I was happy this happened (although it was definitely an accident), because it meant more Codeine prescriptions. I complained immediately about numbness in my arms, constant dizziness and nausea, and the inability to walk due to severe pain in my left leg, and was told "the pain is all in your head." The doctors—none of whom knew that I was addicted to opiate and benzodiazepine pills but were aware of my severe stress at home—attributed the pain to stress. There was definitely some truth to that. However, years later, at the very beginning of my recovery, I met Dr. Scott Rosa, DC, who specializes in spinal-cord and brain-injury cases and is world-renowned for his work with Image Guided Atlas Treatment, where former NFL quarterback Jim McMahon successfully sought help for his injuries. Dr. Rosa used his imaging and treatment and found that, in my accidental fall in 2003, I had sustained a spinal-cord injury as well as brain lesions, which went untreated until we met in 2013. Dr. Rosa has been a godsend to me, and I was in his care for seven years, up until 2020. I live with ongoing pain and structural challenges, but now, I live my life successfully with intermittent Atlas treatments as needed, in conjunction with my healthy self care practices. (See more about Dr. Rosa at http://rosaclinic.com/.)

In 2006, after years of living with me in my chronic and progressive disease (not fully realizing it was the addiction), an immediate family member said to me at that time, "Don't you see what a burden you are to myself and to your children?" This family member did not know how to help me, and convinced me to end my life with a bottle of five hundred codeine sulfate pills that I had just refilled at the pharmacy. I was not in a lucid mindset. I was helpless, hopeless, and vulnerable, and I felt guilty about what my family was going through.

I did not know who to ask for help for my SUD at that time, and saw no other way out, and so I agreed. I wrote goodbye letters to my children and gave them to this person. We said our goodbyes, and he went into the living room to await my passing. As I lay there, I wanted to die only because I couldn't see a way out, and I had no support. I feared facing the untreated, very painful, existing trauma. It was the thought and visualization of my children standing over my coffin that stopped me from taking those pills with the intention of ending my life. Years later in early 2013, after awakening from a lethal overdose, my children and the thought of their suffering, and again envisioning them standing over my coffin is what gave me the strength to ask for help to save my life. I wanted to change the trajectory of my legacy. I was able to have that awareness in a moment of Divine intervention in between swallowing handfuls of pills.

I am now in my ninth year of recovery in the year 2021.

About a year into my recovery, I said to the family member who had encouraged me to die by suicide, "You wanted me to kill myself, and look at me now." He said, "I know." That was his only response. I never got an apology. He was never able to connect with me emotionally, and I am aware that he saw no other way out for any of us. He lacked the coping skills. I hold no ill will toward him. He did all that he knew how to do at that time with the tools that he had available to him. He was probably terrified, watching me slowly dying over the years. Beyond all doubt, I know that he loved me in his own way. We all deal with pain, suffering, loss, and disease with the tools that we have at hand, and we do the best that we can at the time.

By the grace of God, I survived.

Look up child…

The Limits of Traditional Medicine

During my active addiction, I was able to manipulate a handful of doctors, and one pharmacy, to prescribe in excess of two thousand pills a month, which nearly took my life quite a few times. I have learned that I am ultimately responsible for my choices in life. However, when I was beyond incoherent and knocking at death's door, where were the doctors and this pharmacy? They were not there, trying to save my life. They believed they were helping me. They believed that all problems could be solved with medication, so they kept giving me pills to "help" me. The amounts were lethal; they gave me whatever I wanted, in any amount that I wanted with no questions. No fuss. How did they get away with this type of reckless behavior?

The Hippocratic Oath that healthcare professionals swear to says that they will "practice medicine honestly." Furthermore, they will "maintain the highest principles of moral, ethical, and legal conduct." Wouldn't Hippocrates be shocked at the way so many of our healthcare professionals, and much of our entire healthcare system, have become not only dishonest but full of reckless behavior that is endangering the members of our society, or even killing them? WHERE IS THEIR ACCOUNTABILITY? Well, in my story, the doctor writing the prescriptions was a drug-addiction "specialist," and psychiatrist. He is no longer practicing medicine, as I filed a complaint in 2014, and his license was permanently revoked in September, 2018. The following list of prescriptions were all filled at the same pharmacy (who, in my opinion, were equally reckless in unquestioningly dispensing the medications as the physician was in writing them). Below is a "sobering" snapshot of the pharmacy records from March 4, 2009 through April 22, 2009. As I review this list, I am in disbelief, even all of these years later, that I received the following prescriptions and filled them all at the same pharmacy, and that I lived to tell about it. I had been using this pharmacy for twenty-plus years. I felt we were like "family," but they never intervened to try to save my life.

(* Signifies that it was the same doctor writing the prescriptions.)

*03/04/09 IBUPROFEN 800MG QTY: 50

*03/04/09 DONNATOL 16.2MG QTY: 100

*03/06/09 HYDROMORPHON QTY: 4MG

*03/6/09 CODEINE SULF 60MG QTY: 350

*03/06/19 TRIMETHOBENZ 300MG QTY: 50

*03/10/09 CYCLOBENZAPR 10MG QTY: 90

03/12/09 CHLORD/CLIDI 5-2.5MG QTY: 90

*03/19/09 CODEINE SULFATE 60MG QTY: 400

*03/19/09 ALPRAZOLAM 2MG QTY: 150

03/19/09 PROCRIT 20,000/ML QTY: 6

*03/20/09 IBUPROFEN 800MG QTY: 50

*03/23/09 HYDROMORPHON 4MG QTY: 90

*04/1/09 IBUPROFEN 800MG QTY: 50

*04/02/09 HYDROMORPHON 4MG QTY: 90

*04/02/09 ALPRAZOLAM 2MG QTY: 100

*04/06/09 DONNATOL 16.2MG QTY: 100

*04/06/09 TRIMETHOBENZ 300MG QTY: 50

04/11/09 FLUTICASONE 50MCG QTY: 16

04/11/09 CHLORPROMAZ 25MG QTY: 30

*04/12/09 CODEINE SULF 60MG QTY: 400

*04/18/09 IBUPROFEN 800MG QTY: 50

*04/22/09 HYDROMORPHONE 4MG QTY: 90

*04/22/09 ALPRAZOLAM 2MG QTY: 150

*04/22/09 IBUPROFEN 800MG QTY: 50

I am a mother, grandmother, friend, teacher, human being, and precious soul. My accountability for my actions ceased when I was incoherent and no longer in charge of my faculties. I was in a drug-induced psychosis. Among other things, I believed my husband was trying to kill me, that he was involved in heinous murders, that people were spying on me through my computer and stereo speakers, and that the TV shows that I was watching were using my name to talk to me directly (and I answered them). I shared all of this with the "addiction psychiatrist" to no avail. He wrote it down but never questioned me further, and in fact, many times toward the end of my active addiction, I didn't even go to his office, because I was too ill to leave home. He simply called the pharmacy with refill after refill, any time I made a request. The pharmacy filled each one. The pharmacist used to ask me to pay cash so she wouldn't have to "put it through the system." And I did. And she did her thing.

I could not think about anything but making sure I had enough drugs in my purse and in my home every day. I ate, slept, and breathed drugs, continuing to self-medicate to escape the memories and the pain of the past. And at that time, my tolerance level had become very high-dangerously high. I needed more and more pills, up to 30 or more per day, to feel that same "high" that previously required only 2 or 3 pills to achieve that same feeling.

At that time, when I was in active disease, medication dispensing was not monitored the way it is today. Unfortunately, there are still many reckless prescribers who are literally "getting away with murder." At least once a week, I hear tragic story after tragic story—same story... different person. I have learned that substance use disorder is a chronic and progressive brain disease related to our DNA (our genetic "family tree"). It is also impacted by our environment, and how well we are practicing daily self care. However, this disease is diagnosable, treatable, and manageable. Recovery and wellness are spectacular when you commit to them, but you have to want it and crave it more than you crave anything else. Much of the time, those living with SUD, a brain disorder, are unable to understand the potentially lethal dynamics of what they are experiencing. They may be experiencing a co-occurring disorder, (a second disorder occurring simultaneously) a mental illness like depression, where they use drugs, alcohol, or use unhealthy behaviors to self medicate. They do not have the presence of mind to identify what they are feeling, so, they remain on this vicious hamster wheel of self-destruction. Loved ones do not have the legal right to force treatment onto their loved one living with these disorders. This is one of the most frustrating dilemmas for families, and certainly, for the person living with these disorders.

For me, Divine clarity broke through this cycle, and I knew I would have to be willing to begin new healthy practices, and to address the PTSD (post-traumatic stress disorder) I experienced in relation to the ongoing trauma I had endured in my life. I have learned to live and to thrive holistically, and that is what I am doing: thriving!

We depend upon our medical community to take care of us according to the oath they have taken as doctors, pharmacists, and healthcare providers. Yet not one doctor whose care I was under questioned me about any suspicions they may have had. When I finally asked for help, my primary-care physician said that he had "suspected" that I was addicted to my medications, yet he had never confronted me in all of the years I was his patient. I do not blame him. In fact, today, and for all of the years in my recovery, he has been one of my greatest cheerleaders. Recently, he called me a "rockstar." This meant so much to me to have his validation. Many of those in the medical community simply lack knowledge, awareness, and education on this disease. Happily, many that I speak to in the medical community are willing to be educated and empowered, so that they may be a part of the solution in fighting this disease.

Now vs. Then

In my opinion, recovery from SUD, and co-occurring disorders, is not about how much time I have not used substances or keeping track of my "recovery date." It's not about keeping score of the days gone by. I celebrate the yearly milestone of my wellness, but it is more about the life lessons that I've experienced in my recovery that enhances the "new normal" I have created in my life. I embrace life day-to-day, using all of the tools that I have acquired in order to live my truth. I am resilient when I meet with adversity and challenge. I measure my successful recovery at the end of the day by evaluating my strengths and challenges, and what I can use tomorrow as a tool to continue to evolve and to thrive. And, As I practice balance in all that I do, I feel steady on my feet, and continue to "walk the talk" on my path, and to humbly pay it forward.

Even when writing this book, one of my editor's at the time, Keidi Keating, told me that I was "holding back details," and in order to connect with the reader, would need to go back and rewrite with specifics. This very task, once again, caused triggers that escalated my anxiety; however, because I have done so much work on healing, I surrounded myself with my self-care tools each time I would sit down to rewrite and felt safe and in control.

Every day since I decided to live, I have learned new ways of healing through natural and organic solutions and using an integrative approach to recovery. The more I learn, the more eager I am to keep learning and collecting tools for myself, and to help others. *Today I am the healthiest I have ever been.*

I surround myself with a team of healthcare professionals, both traditional and holistic, and we work together to find a balance of treatment techniques that will be of the highest benefit to my wellness. I make the final call. No controlled substances. This is non-negotiable. I was finally ready to explore the root problems that made me want to be in a mind-altered, numb state of being. And it all began with a prayer to God. With God's love, grace, and guidance giving me strength, I took that first step. I spoke my truth about my addiction. Then, taking baby steps when I was ready, I continued on my path. *I was finally free.* I had earned a sense of pride and accomplishment. Success. I began feeling energetic, alive, healthy, and clear. It had me wanting more success in the healing process. With all of this came commitment to my wellness. I am completely dedicated to my new lifestyle.

I treat all of my health challenges, including my ongoing anxiety, by managing my symptoms through spiritual solutions and healthy self care practices.

I support my health with a variety of whole foods and plant based vitamins and minerals. I've eliminated sugar—a known anxiety producer—from my diet, as well as processed foods, cow's dairy, gluten, and most grains, unless they are gluten-free. I get outdoors each day for sunlight, which promotes production of Vitamin D, raises dopamine (the happy hormone!) levels naturally, and decreases my anxiety. Despite using a walker in the past, I remain active every day through walking outdoors and/or going to the gym. Exercise supports healing for the "addicted brain," reduces relapse frequency, and in general supports wellness body, mind and spirit. It is a key part of my recovery.

My exercise regimen and my music are my natural "go-to's" for managing symptoms of depression and anxiety. I am sure to have enough rest and sleep each night. An ongoing disruption of sleep can directly affect our mental health. In addition, I eat plenty of tyrosine-rich foods. In order to make dopamine, our bodies need tyrosine, which can be found in almonds, bananas, avocados, eggs, beans, fish, and chicken. Further, I am sure to eat polyphenol rich foods which are referred to as "lifetime essentials." Polyphenol rich foods are the antioxidants in plant foods. They reduce the blood sugar spikes we may experience after meals, as well as chronic inflammation. Finally, I use probiotics to keep my gut healthy as a large percentage of our immune system is housed in our gut. Healthy gut, healthy immune system, healthy mind!

I also stay connected to loved ones and friends every day. Connection is imperative for a successful, lifelong recovery. My daily work in serving others living with these brain disorders also provides me with a great sense of purpose, satisfaction, and gratitude.

I am perhaps most grateful for the Divine blessings the Universe/God/Spirit has sent to me along my journey. God has been so present in my life, and I am truly in awe of how He has guided me to co-create this amazing and blessed life that I now live. I believe that when we are connected to the Universe, we stay in alignment with the highest form of self. "We" have a strong connection for which I am deeply grateful. I am devoted to my spiritual practice in daily meditation and prayer. It is the *foundation* of my recovery.

Each day in prayer, I say, "Please show me where to go, who to see, what to say and to whom to help another person." This is loosely taken from "*A Course In Miracles*", which is a metaphysical text that I have studied and use in my spiritual practice and daily life. My daily prayer is always answered. I ask for strength each day, good health, and for loving guidance in all that I do. I pray for my loved ones' health, safety, and abundance, and for peace for everyone. I practice my faith by trusting that, no matter what is happening in my life, I have a "knowing" that I am protected. I never second guess the Universe's guidance. And, I practice Kundalini meditation, which is said to release kundalini energy at the base of the spine, promoting my communication with the Universe/God/Spirit.

It is a profound experience to find recovery and to be successful, and it becomes even more meaningful when you can share it. You have to be the difference to make a difference. Find those who truly want to know the solution, and share it with love. This is the way that we create change. We begin within, then we share it with others. It becomes a ripple effect that slowly, and purposefully, filters out into our community and into the world, one person at a time.

In this book, I will share my thoughts, my experiences, my memories, and my wisdom through inspirational quotes and writing. As referenced earlier, I have left a space for you to reflect and to write about it, if you read something that resonates with you.

You will notice that I refer to a higher source interchangeably as Universe/God/Spirit. Substitute your own name for the God of your own understanding. I will share with you the prayers, meditations, and affirmations that help me to stay firmly grounded in deep faith throughout my recovery, some of which are offered by my spiritual mentors and teachers, and some of which I have created. I invite you to try them all at least once to explore the possibility of connection to any of them, and then to write your experiences on the space provided, if you so desire. This "journaling" is a way of staying connected to oneself each day, knowing that we are all allowed to feel however we feel, and to allow ourselves to feel it all. Herein lies healing.

I urge you to choose whatever resonates with you and to implement it in your own recovery. Please keep in mind that some people may need to implement other types of self care tools including medication, a visit with a medical professional, a 12 step program, or speaking with a mental health professional. It is always a personal choice, and one's self care tools may change over one's lifetime to accommodate whatever challenges may arise. *You should choose whatever healthy alternatives work for you.*

I do the work. I walk the talk. I am a recovery warrior, and I love to share what I have experienced in order to serve others. Mine is an untapped pathway to recovery. My "integrative approach to recovery." Follow me into my story of nearly a lifetime, through forty years of prescription-drug addiction and mental health disorders, and into my recovery through spiritual solutions and self-care, where I made a choice to live.

May God/Universe/Spirit bless you on whatever path you choose to travel.

Look up child …

CHAPTER 2

A New Beginning

"Recovery, Rebirth, Release"
Matthew DeGroat

I n early 2013, my son, Matthew, designed a platform for me to write about my recovery from substance use disorder and mental illness. We called the blog and its accompanying website (no longer online) "The Rx Diaries." He came up with the words: "recovery, rebirth, release," and used a butterfly as the focal point of my logo. The butterfly symbol is the perfect depiction of my journey. I have broken free from the darkness, abandoned the chrysalis, and am now free to live in my truth. We have many "rebirths" throughout our lives, and each time, we release whatever no longer serves us. As we shed that skin, we continue to learn, grow, and evolve, and to remain in a state of ease within our truest and highest self. This is where we are also able to offer ourselves fully to helping others on their journey.

Recovery from anything is an ongoing journey, and it is all about what road we choose to travel. There are times when we travel in the darkness, and there are times when we hit a roadblock. In those "in-between moments," we learn resourcefulness and resiliency in waiting out the darkness, knowing that the sun will always come out tomorrow. For me, I chose the road less travelled, yet I have never lost my way. It is said that everyone loves a comeback story. This is especially true for a woman who "came back swinging" from a life of substance use disorder and co-occurring mental health disorders. I am a woman with an inspirational story to share that offers hope to others struggling with this disease. I wrote. I prayed. I recovered through discipline, determination, and persistence in practicing spiritual solutions and self-care … and through these practices, this book—this labor of love that I am sharing—was born:

WRITE PRAY RECOVER: A JOURNEY TO WELLNESS THROUGH SPIRITUAL SOLUTIONS AND SELF-CARE.

Before we begin, I want to say an extra special, "Thank you," to my devoted, loving, and supportive son, Matthew, for being my greatest cheerleader and supporter, encouraging me through every step of my recovery, and for being my best friend. My son is deeply empathetic and compassionate (He always says, "Just like you, Mom.") and has forgiven the years of hardship that he endured due to my addiction, mental illness, and the poor choices associated with an unwell body, mind, and spirit. All of my children have rallied around me in my recovery with deep love and encouragement, and it is in great part due to their devotion and forgiveness that I have made such extraordinary progress in my wellness. I am finally the mom they deserve to have. I feel so blessed each time I hear one of my precious children call me "Mom." I am living up to what this endearing term means to us all: unconditional love in a safe, non-judgmental space, providing joyous and meaningful experiences, loving guidance when asked, and intermittent unsolicited but well-meaning insight. A mom is someone who stands beside her children through every storm, and offers choices and solutions while allowing her children to make the ultimate decision (in their own time) as to what is best for them individually. Most importantly, a mom steadfastly stands in the space of love, compassion, peace, and eagerness to live each and every moment with passion and authenticity. It was the thought of my children, Matthew, Nicole, Olivia, and Sarah, and my deep love for them, in that Divinely led moment, that gave me an indescribable strength to speak my truth in asking for help to save my life.

Here is my story…

On April 2, 2013, I got ready for bed, and in a moment where I had some clarity in between swallowing handfuls of pills, I dropped to my knees and asked God to help me to save my life. I told Him that if He could show me the way out of this, I would devote my life to any path He put before me. At the end of my prayer, I said, "In the next song on the radio, please give me a sign that you are with me." I sat down on the edge of my bed, turned on the radio, and the first song to play was "Jesus, Take the Wheel," by Carrie Underwood. The words touched my heart, and I became so emotional. I went to bed knowing that I would soon be given specific guidance from the Universe that would save my life. The next morning I heard a strong, intuitive voice say to me, "Call for help. It is time." I heard this voice tell me, "Everything is going to be alright." I have been listening to that voice ever since. That day, my life was saved by the grace of God.

Since that time, I have been physically and mentally recovering through spiritual solutions and self care practices. I have been recovering through working with a team of spiritual advisors. I have also been studying the teachings of Gabby Bernstein, Brene Brown, Iyanla Vanzant, DeVon Franklin, Wayne Dyer, Deepak Chopra, and other world-renowned spiritual teachers and motivational and transformational teachers/leaders. I have studied the metaphysical text, *A Course In Miracles*, and through its text, have also learned new perspectives and thought patterns. I have also studied and now practice, Dialectical Behavioral Therapy (DBT), which is a form of Cognitive Behavioral Therapy (CBT). DBT helps one to "identify and positively change negative thinking patterns" and offers successful outcomes.

A Course In Miracles teaches that a "*miracle is a shift in perception.*" This is where we come from a place of openness and willingness to create change to enhance our lives. A miracle is where we are open to seeing a different perspective from a place of love and forgiveness of ourselves and others—a "shift in perception."

I am deeply aware that I must never take my disease for granted, as it is always waiting to come out of hiding, and it is easily triggered. This disease will tell me to "try the high" one more time, and so I must always remain mindful of my disease. I must remain The Warrior. I do this by practicing spiritual solutions and self-care many times throughout each day. When my body asks to rest, I rest. When my mind asks for some quiet time, I oblige. My wellness is the most important thing to me. Spirit is the source of my strength, and where I receive my daily guidance for experiencing wellness.

Inherently, we all know what we need to heal. We must offer ourselves that space of healing. If we are connected to our inner self, we will be aware of what our body, mind, and spirit needs to thrive in every moment. It is a choice. It ripples out into caring for my family, my clients, and my community.

Through the experience of love and forgiveness, and openness to experiencing and practicing new perspectives, the miracle occurs. And, we experience wellness body, mind and spirit.

This is the reason I am blessed to share my journey, freely, unabashedly, unapologetically, and proudly, with the intention of serving others.

Recovery will look different for each of us: in-patient treatment, outpatient treatment, therapy, twelve-step recovery, holistic recovery, or whatever else we ourselves know we need in order to heal. In addition, we must make changes in which we practice ongoing commitment to a new and healthy lifestyle. I have learned that we must let go of expectations. A moment of trying your best is your only expectation in recovery. Create a new healthy and sustainable lifestyle. Hold yourself accountable for that. Stand deeply in your faith—whatever "faith" means or looks like for you—and expect that your recovery will have ups and downs. Recovery, as in life, is not linear.

We all have mental health, and our mental and physical health are directly connected. Substance Use Disorder (SUD) is a mental illness. Sometimes, on the continuum, we feel well, and sometimes we feel unwell, depending upon what's going on within us and around us. Our environment, our biological factors, and even our self-care, impacts our wellness. It is up to us to be aware of our own signs and symptoms as we begin to feel unwell, and of what we need in order to move back to wellness. Inherently, we all know what we need to heal, and it will be different for everyone. It may change over one's lifetime. We must practice prevention in removing ourselves from anything toxic, including foods, thoughts, and relationships. Most importantly, we must know that, when we have done all of that, we may move ourselves back to wellness, and if we aren't successful, we must understand that asking for professional help is a healthy decision and the highest form of self-care. When we are unwell physically, and remain unwell for an extended period of time, we go to the doctor. We must practice the same type of self-care when it applies to our mental health. Healthy practices—body, mind, and spirit—promote wellness.

Self-care is the actions that we take to achieve wellness, and wellness is where we stand in our power!

Wishing you harmonious health for life!

When you begin to feel unwell mentally, what are the physical signs and symptoms that offer you this information? Which healthy practices help you to cope with these issues?

_____

_____

_____

_____

_____

_____

_____

What types of preventative self care have you tried in the past? Which ones were helpful? How did they help you? Which seemed less helpful? Is there any way they might be modified to be more effective for you?

_____

_____

_____

_____

_____

_____

_____

Of the types of self care presented in this chapter, which seem like they could be beneficial to you? If needed, do you know of any professionals who might be able to guide you in applying them to your life to create new ways of coping with stress?

_____

_____

_____

_____

_____

_____

_____

What spiritual books have you read? Which were especially meaningful to you? Write about it. Are there any that would be worth rereading to help you stay focused on your wellness?

_____

_____

_____

_____

_____

_____

_____

_____

CHAPTER 3
Dreams Do Come True

"Truth is my name/I am truth"

- Sat Nam

S ince I began my recovery in early 2013, my dream has been to travel around the country on a speaking tour where I can be the facilitator of a dialogue that is so necessary pertaining to substance use disorder and mental illness. Having an open and ongoing dialogue is vital to understanding and normalizing these disorders, reducing stigma, educating communities, raising awareness, and offering the proper care to those affected (and their loved ones). Those who live with SUD deserve the same love, respect, kindness, and empathy received by anyone with any other disease. I believe that my dream is slowly coming to fruition.

From the onset of my recovery, I have given many successful presentations, trainings, and speeches on SUD and mental health recovery locally and state-wide, and most recently in 2021, internationally. Each presentation that I give is emotional for me. I know that I am making a small difference in opening up the dialogue on these disorders that have been "hushed" for too long. And the silence has become deafening. I am proud of my recovery as I look back to see how far I have come, how much I have grown, and all that I have learned and accomplished. Each time I stand up in front of an audience to speak, I am completely embraced as I stand in my truth, and it is so humbling for me. I am overcome with gratitude—gratitude for a second chance, and for learning a completely new and healthy lifestyle.

After each presentation, there are so many people who come to speak with me to tell me about their own struggles (or a loved one's struggle) with substance use disorder and mental illness. This is why I do the work that I do. So many people tell me they have never talked about this before. The more we talk about this, the more we normalize the symptoms of these disorders, the more people will realize that there is no shame in being unwell. We will forever be rid of the stigma of of these chronic and progressive brain disorders. The work that I do is so empowering. Education is key. It lets others know that these disorders are diagnosable, treatable, and manageable, and that they are not alone. It assures them that we are all worthy of the best care in recovery, regardless of the type of disease you are living with and navigating.

I have found my passion: helping others through my lived experience.

Start where you are. Honor yourself. Honor your own gorgeous individual path. Proudly stand in your own gorgeous truth.

Prayers, Meditations, And Practitioners Who Serve And/Or Teach and Inspire at A Glance

A Prayer for Loving Guidance

My recovery, as I've mentioned, is grounded in my spiritual practices of daily prayer and meditation. I began this practice while in active substance use disorder, and it was the one small, yet profound, daily practice that helped to keep me connected to Spirit. When I would begin to feel the urge to take a handful of pills, or to engage in self-harming behavior, I would pray for loving guidance and strength. Even if I was only able to take fewer pills after my prayer, or wait an extra thirty minutes before I engaged in self-harming behavior, I felt I was being Divinely supported. After I had taken a lethal number of pills and feel my heart begin to race, and knew there was a chance I could have a heart attack and/or die, I would pray to God to save my life. I did not really want to die; I was just so ill and drug dependent, and I did not know how to stop, or where to go to ask for help. I would say The Serenity Prayer over and over, aloud, down on my knees. I would also repeat it sometimes as I sat on my bedroom floor, looking up at the sky, crying tears of sorrow for the life I was abusing (and quickly losing)—mine and tears for those of my loved ones who were watching helplessly from the sidelines as I was slowly dying.

"God, grant me the serenity to accept the things I cannot change, the courage to change the things I can, and the wisdom to know the difference."

Once I began my recovery, I discovered Kundalini meditation, which is known as the "yoga of awareness" through which one may awaken to one's higher self. The higher self is the enlightened part of ourselves that is connected to the Universe/God/Spirit. I continue this practice daily to remain connected throughout each moment of my day.

Please use any or all of these prayers/meditations as they resonate with you.

The following is a prayer I created in my early recovery:

"Dearest enlightening, loving Spirits and angels of the highest blessings,

I see beyond my physical sight when I am present. I hear beyond my physical hearing when I am open. When I allow myself to receive in a loving space, I am limitless. I listen for your words as I ask for guidance each day, and I follow your wisdom. I feel your presence inside of me and all around me that is all encompassing love. I am so grateful to have your loving guidance. Thank you for my Divine gift of connection, and for all of my blessings. Please continue to keep me deeply grounded in faith, and show me where to go, who to see, what to say and to whom, to help another soul.

My spiritual teachers/advisors and holistic health team/mentors offer a variety of mantras, sutras, meditations, information, and alternative healing practices through natural and organic solutions as I do in my practice. You may connect with any or all of them by visiting the following websites:

Sheila Pearl, MSW Certified Life and Relationship Coach, Spiritual Advisor, Author/Speaker - https://pearl.atomconnects.com

Keidi Keating, Author/Editor
https://www.yourbookangel.com

Alex McRoberts - Yoga Teacher, Certified Life Coach, entrepreneur, podcaster, and Ontario Certified Teacher -
https://www.themindfullifepractice.com

Emily Ruaux - Spiritual Advisor - www.sacredspace.co.uk

Gabby Bernstein - International Spiritual Teacher & Inspirational Speaker/Author www.gabbybernstein.com

Abraham Hicks - Inspirational Speaker/Author
http://www.abraham-hicks.com/lawofattractionsource/index.php

Dr. Wayne Dyer - International Spiritual Motivational/Inspirational Teacher https://www.drwaynedyer.com

Neale Donald Walsch - International Spiritual Speaker/Author http://www.nealedonaldwalsch.com

Louise Hay - Motivational Author https://www.louisehay.com

Deepak Chopra - International Spiritual/Motivational Speaker/Author www.deepakchopra.com

Dr. Brene Brown - Research Professor/Storyteller
https://brenebrown.com/about/

Jill Lawrence Health Coach/Holistic Nutritionist
https://jilllawrencehealth.com

Dr. Zazu Cioce D P T https://www.phoenixpt.info

Dr. Scott Rosa D.C., B.C.A.O. http://rosaclinic.com

Scott Berliner, Pharmacist https://lifesciencepharmacy.com

How do you connect to the Universe/God/Spirit/your higher self?

_____

_____

_____

_____

_____

What are you willing to try as a new practice?

_____

_____

_____

_____

What do you want to experience as part of your spiritual connection and practice? What does that look like, feel like, sound like? How do you see a spiritual practice of your own understanding enhancing your life?

_____

_____

_____

_____

_____

CHAPTER 4
Self-Care

**"Self-Care Is the Actions That We Take To Achieve Wellness
And Wellness Is Where We Stand In Our Power."**

We are all living in a highly stressful world with so many demands on our precious time. Stress builds up in our bodies, and if we don't find ways to manage it, and to help it to move through our cellular structure, it settles on the inside of our bodies, causing us to become diseased.

It is vital for us to be mindful of all that we are doing each day, and to make sure that we choose what is best for us. For so many, there is non-stop rushing through the day, from the moment we open our eyes until we are able to go to sleep at night, and often, that sleep is not restful. After some time, this running and doing for others, going to work, and meeting the everyday challenges of living, we become overwhelmed, super busy and distracted, and we forget to take care of ourselves. We forget to practice self-love and self-care.

Think of it as you would your bank account. You must continue to replenish your bank account as your bills come in each month, otherwise your account becomes depleted, or even bankrupt. You must think of your wellness account in the same way! We have so many demands on our time and energy each day. If we do not replenish our wellness account, and we continue to "give out" our energy to all of the demands, we will go into debt, energetically, and become physically, mentally and spiritually bankrupt.

We stay ahead of the stress by practicing self care. Self care is our best tool for awareness and prevention of developing a mental health disorder, or exacerbating an existing disorder. Self care builds the capacity for us to deal with stress and not become depleted.

I wake up every day before dawn. Before I do anything, I do an "oil pulling" technique to rid my body of all the toxins that may have built up overnight, making their way from my gut into my mouth. Oil pulling is an ancient Ayurvedic technique that dates back three thousand years. Gently swish one tablespoon of coconut oil around in your mouth for about fifteen minutes. This will "pull" out the toxins. Once you are done, spit it into the garbage pail. *NEVER SWALLOW IT OR SPIT IT DOWN THE DRAIN.* Brush and floss as usual. I also "pull" at night before bed.

Next, I drink a warm glass of lemon water to further detoxify, and then engage in meditation and prayer, coffee in hand (or a relaxing tea), for thirty to sixty minutes. I take my time in the shower, allowing the very warm water to run down my body, lathering up, rinsing, and then allowing the cold water to run for about a minute. This feeling is so invigorating and wakes up all of my senses. And it makes me smile! I am sending a message to my brain and to my body that I am awake and happy!

During my hour of self-care, I also write my blog with my favorite music playing in the background. Through Spirit, and using my own lived experiences, I "hear" so much that needs to be communicated, and in addition to being very cathartic for me, it may also serve others seeking some daily inspiration. Throughout my day, each and every day, I am inspired by experiences, people, and places that I encounter, and immediately want to share. It is through this sharing, I believe, that I weave my thread into the fabric of others, and we connect and create a gorgeous collective tapestry.

I then prepare a healthy, organic meal. I sit and eat mindfully, tasting each bite, chewing thoroughly, swallowing slowly, and always in gratitude. I sit in awe of the Universe as I look out my window at the gorgeous view of the trees and sky as the sun is rising. My heart is soaring and open with so much gratitude for my blessings. I am deeply grateful for being given a second chance to live. It is extraordinary. It is a miracle.

We must make the time for ourselves, through healthy practices, to experience wellness. I see so many people pushed to their limit, who choose to eat on the run, stopping at fast-food restaurants to find "food" to give them fuel to keep on going. The fuel from fast foods is merely "fumes." I have seen an epidemic of unhealthy, chronic moods developing in our world: anger, impatience, anxiety, depression, etc.

Stress, poor nutrition, being unhappy in one's career and/or relationships, lack of exercise, poor sleep hygiene, and no spiritual practice, in my opinion, are the underlying factors of this unhealthy mood epidemic.

Scientifically, we have learned that the foods we eat directly affect our moods. The food/mood relationship is maintained by neurotransmitters, which are chemical messengers that relay thoughts and actions throughout the brain. Dopamine and serotonin are produced primarily in our gut, which is where our second brain resides—in the lining of our gut. Our "gut brain" and our actual brain constantly communicate with each other. They are connected physically and chemically. If we are feeding our gut—where our necessary neurotransmitters are produced for good mental health and overall wellness—with unhealthy, toxic food and substances, and experiencing ongoing stress, and living in a chronically unhealthy mood of anger, worry, depression, it represses the production of these neurotransmitters. The brain is not receiving the neurotransmitters it needs for good mental health and psychological vigor!

Research has shown that unhealthy changes in our gut microbiome and gut inflammation can affect the brain and promote symptoms that look like mental illness, Parkinson's disease, and even Autism.

Some neurotransmitters, such as serotonin (which can make us feel relaxed), and others, such as dopamine, have a stimulating effect. Food breaks down in our digestive tract and enters our bloodstream, which creates changes in the behavior of these neurotransmitters and impacts our mood. We know that whatever we eat either promotes inflammation or promotes wellness on a cellular level. Add the junk food to the stresses of everyday life, unhappiness in career and relationships, no compass for spirituality, poor sleep hygiene, dehydration, ingesting toxic substances, and a myriad of other unhealthy practices, and we have a recipe for disease.

Taking at least 30 minutes a day for self-care is imperative for refueling naturally. Here are some easy self-care tools/actions that I use, and that you can use as well if they resonate with you:

- Prepare a healthy meal for yourself at home with "nutrient-dense" whole foods. "A nutrient-dense food has lots of nutrients with little calories. You want to look for foods that are rich in vitamins, minerals, complex carbohydrates, lean protein and healthy fats." This includes greens, protein, healthier types of gluten-free grains such as amaranth, millet, or quinoa, and plenty of water to detox all of the everyday toxins that our bodies absorb. Eat slowly, calmly, joyfully, stress free, and with a mindful purpose. Practice gratitude for your amazing, healthy meal.

- Take a 20 minute detox bath with 1 cup of epsom salts or dead sea salt, 1/2 cup of baking soda, and 1/2 cup of apple cider vinegar. Put them into a tub of hot water and add in your preference of essential oils. Soak for 10- 20 minutes, and be sure to stay hydrated throughout your soak by drinking water. You need to stay hydrated during your bath, as well as post detox bath for 24 hours. As a rule, drink plenty of water throughout the day, every day.

- Enjoy a cup of chamomile tea, matcha tea, lavender tea, or whatever tea is relaxing to you.

- Light your favorite candles.

- Listen to relaxing sounds (Gong bath, rain, ocean waves)

- Do some gentle stretches to awaken your body and your mind.

- Take a quiet walk.

- Spend time with family and friends.

- Journal, free write, sketch.

- Disconnect from social media, texts, cell phone, etc. (Be brave! Try it!) I love the sound of silence.

- Connect to the Universe/God/Spirit, or whatever spiritual practice you subscribe to, every day. It is how I stay grounded and the way in which I enhance my awareness.

- Connecting with loved ones, even if they have passed on or if we are estranged. I give and receive love through prayer and *kything*, which is a "communion skill, a Spirit-to-Spirit loving presence which can bring about a deep sense of peace and communication." I do this as a daily practice. My spiritual practices offer me love and connection. The more love that we send out into the world, the more love we receive. And we thrive when we are loved!

Thoughts on Self-Care:

Take care of yourself as you take care of others. You are the most important person in your life. Give yourself the gift of time to explore the things that are good for you, make you happy, and will enhance your life. Without you being in the best state of whole healthiness and harmony, nothing else matters.

Sometimes, even practicing self-care can be challenging when we are feeling unwell emotionally and physically. It is always okay to do absolutely nothing but rest, sleep, watch TV, cry, or allow yourself to experience your feelings. You do not have to move forward every day. Sometimes giving yourself permission to "stand still" is the most empathetic self-care you can offer yourself.

Tomorrow is another day to try again. When I feel sad and a bit disconnected, I say this little prayer to myself: *"Today, I know that what I need is peace, silence, reflection, and solitude. I offer that to myself for today as my self-care practice."*

Then I make myself my favorite coffee or tea, pray for strength and comfort, tune into my body, mind, and spirit, and offer myself what I know will be healing for me today, whatever that looks like and feels like in each and every moment of this day.

Ask your own intuition for guidance. Ask Spirit for guidance. Allow yourself to connect. Achieve wellness in your own time, and in whatever way is healing for *you*.

ASK, ALLOW, ACHIEVE.

Let your own intuition be your guide. Baby steps. Just for this moment. Self-care is the actions that we take to achieve wellness, and wellness is where we stand in our power!

How do you practice self-love and self-care? What resonates with you? What are you willing to try as a new practice today?

_____

_____

_____

_____

_____

_____

Try it daily for one week. How did you feel afterwards? If it served you, try it for sixty-six days. Research shows us that when we implement a new healthy practice for sixty-six days, it becomes a new healthy lifestyle habit! Write about it at the end of the sixty-six days. Describe what you have observed during this time, the changes that you may have experienced, and how this practice has enhanced your life.

_____

_____

_____

_____

_____

_____

_____

_____

How has your relationship with food changed? What have you observed about your wellness, including your mental health since you have implemented these changes?

_____

_____

_____

_____

_____

_____

_____

What have you added to your spiritual practice? What have you observed about your wellness, including your mental health since you have implemented these changes?

_____

_____

_____

_____

_____

_____

_____

_____

What steps have you taken to improve any unhealthy/toxic relationships? Environments? Other unhealthy/toxic practices?

_____

_____

_____

_____

_____

_____

_____

_____

_____

_____

CHAPTER 5
When You Believe

"When all hope is gone, have faith."

I love the Spiritual warrior that I have become. In my world, I believe that we are guided and protected by angels, enlightened, loving, guiding Spirits, our departed loved ones, and mentors who have transitioned to a higher plane. I believe they are beings of light and energy who lead us and support us as we navigate our paths every day. I believe that these Divine guides surround us all, and that all we have to do is ask for support, guidance, or answers in order to receive it. Whatever noun it is that resonates with you to describe your interpretation of a higher energy, that is where you will find your spiritual strength, connection, guidance, and peace.

We, of course, have free will to engage with our loving, enlightened, guiding Spirits who are always available and around us. Some believe it is God who speaks to us, some the Universe, some Spirit, and some just a vague "Source." I believe we are all one, a collective consciousness of interconnected energy made up of billions of seemingly distinct people or souls in any form that our spirit takes. Some say that Einstein said, "Everything is energy and that's all there is to it. Match the frequency of the reality you want and you cannot help but get that reality. It can be no other way. This is not philosophy. This is physics." Some say it wasn't Einstein who coined this, but hey, it definitely makes sense!

And…This is not for everyone.

I used to be a skeptic, like many people, until I noticed signs that were so definitive—signs I hadn't even asked for—that could not be ignored. I couldn't help but pay attention. I began to look and listen beyond my physical sight and hearing, and tuned into this deep feeling in the pit of my stomach when I knew something to be true. Chills also accompany this gut feeling that I receive in the quiet of meditation, in songs that play with a specific theme, and in many other creative ways that our loving angels and guides use to communicate with all of us if we are open to a dialogue. Even through technology!

My mother passed away on March 20, 2020, and on Mother's Day of 2021, I had been talking to her, praying to her, and missing her deeply. As I stood up from my couch to walk into my kitchen, I noticed in my peripheral vision a dark red object at my front window. When I turned to look, it was a cardinal! I had never seen one in living color before, only in pictures! Cardinals are known to appear when departed loved ones are sending messages that they hear us, and are around us. I quickly took a picture, and watched as this gorgeous bird looked at me, hopping from branch to branch for about five minutes, and then flew off. It was a sign. My mom had heard my words to her. She was communicating with me energetically. My spiritual advisor, Brett, did a reading for me in January, 2021, and said she "saw cardinals and bluebirds" around me. Amen.

There have been times when I would not trust the information I received, and my lack of faith would block my connection. Recently, during a difficult time in my life, I began to doubt my connection to the Universe, and I began to notice a disconnection from God. I felt lost and alone, and so I began to increase my meditation and prayer practice, and asked that the Universe renew our relationship, which is what keeps me grounded every single moment of the day.

I do feel drawn to my loving angels and guides, and I do believe that, when we ask for this relationship, the Universe offers us more love, connection, peace, and joy than we ever experience alone and in isolation.

If this resonates with you, ask for your angels/guides to provide you with information that helps you to navigate your life in your best interest, with highest blessings, and which will protect you. These will be signs that you will completely understand without any doubt, and they will reveal themselves through information, conversations, music, numbers, readings, and a variety of other modalities. This includes simultaneous synchronicities through text messages or emails, through a conversation between others that we may overhear, and many other ways that these beautiful Spirits can get your attention. Ask them for a clear sign that only you would understand as a validation of this Divine relationship and presence, and pay close attention. God/Spirit/ Universe speaks to us in the most curious yet direct ways, especially when Spirit has been trying to reach us, to no avail, to save our life.

In 2012, I was using prescription drugs heavily and had been for quite some time. I was barely able to stay awake every day or function in a normal capacity. I had been getting strong intuitive messages that I would die if I kept going at the rate of ingesting more than two thousand pills a month. I just could not stop. My brain was so unwell. I was living with multi occurring disorders. And … I loved being high. There it is. My truth. My "safety zone" from the years of suppressed emotions.

On October 29, 2012, was the day that Hurricane Sandy was to come through our area. I drove to the pharmacy, after speaking with the pharmacist on the phone and being told to "come down" and that my prescription would be ready. Because of the bad weather, I wanted to make sure that I had plenty of pills in case we lost power, or streets were blocked and I couldn't get to the pharmacy. It is said that when God wants to get your attention, He taps you on the shoulder. If you do not respond, He then gets closer and whispers in your ear. Still no response? He hits you right over the head. Or very nearly, purposefully missing you by a nanosecond. Amen.

The wind-driven rain was blowing across the highway as I drove home from the pharmacy only a mile down the road. The wind was howling, and as I turned off of Route 304, and into my driveway, I pushed the button to open my garage door from the inside of the car so that I could just pull in and stay dry. The garage opened, I pulled in, closed the garage door, and walked through the door that goes from the garage into my downstairs family room. Within three seconds—three, two, one—"BOOM!," I heard a loud crash right outside that shook the ground and the entire house. The lights went out. My precious dog, Max, ran into my arms, barking incessantly. My heart was beating so loudly and fiercely that I could hear it beating in my ears and felt my chest pounding and filling with fright. I was terrified! What the hell had just happened?! I took Max and went into the closet that was located underneath the staircase. We stayed there for about 30 minutes. When I was assured that all was quiet around me and I had calmed down, I went to the front door to see what had happened.

Three trees had crashed down to the ground at the top of our driveway less than twenty-seconds after I had pulled in, taking the telephone pole and wires down with it. God had nearly "hit me over the head." This, was my "wake up call." I believe on that day, that event, was divinely orchestrated, because God had desperately been trying to get my attention for years, to no avail. Those trees, telephone pole, and wires were the closest thing He could use to actually "hit me on the head" without actually killing me, in order to get my attention! Looking back, I see it as a metaphor for impending death. God had called, "Lights out, sound off, darkness, and isolation." Had I turned into that driveway just a few seconds later, I would have been killed. God/Spirit/Universe took that opportunity to let me know that He meant serious business. Either I got help or my death would be imminent.

This was a preview. Surrounded by darkness. No way out. My living grave.

I had to ask for help.

This Divine message resonated deeply with me. I knew I was running out of time. I was trapped in the house with Max. I couldn't get my car out of the garage. There was no power, and I was too weak and too unwell to open the heavy door on my own. My cell phone had about half a bar of power left. I tried to make a call, to no avail. There was no connection. Sinking deeper into the earth. Another "metaphor." I passed out (as usual) from all of the pills, and slept through until morning. Upon awakening, in a moment of clarity, in a moment of hope that God was guiding me and all would be okay, in a moment where I connected with myself and screamed aloud, "I want to live!" I picked up Max in my arms, stood out on the deck of my house in the backyard, and screamed as loud as I could, over and over, "Please help me! I'm trapped!" There were no neighbors on either side of me, and the closest houses were quite a distance from where I was standing on the deck in the neighborhood about a quarter a mile away.

I had been nearly "scared to death," the night before. I was, indeed, living in total darkness, disconnected, and could not see the light. It had been the "perfect storm." Perhaps that was the beginning of my awakening. My "wake up call."

Finally, a neighbor down at the end of my property yelled back, "We've called the police! They are on their way!"

My husband (at that time) and I were going through a divorce, but it was Alan who ultimately came to help us and took us to safety until the debris was cleared. It was going be two weeks before power or heat would be restored, and friends offered me shelter for as long as I needed. However, I wanted to be alone with my pills, my puppy, my pain and my disease. And my disease was in control of my thoughts and behaviors. I wanted to be free to remain numb, and free to be high, and I could not do that in the presence of others.

I wanted to lay in bed, to sleep, and to just "be."

I chose to go home and remain in the very cold, dark environment until my power was restored. My comfort zone. My sanctuary.

My hell and my haven.

Yet, in my fleeting moments of clarity, through my connection to God, I knew that one way or the other, something major was about to shift for me. Through the signs, He had planted the seeds of my recovery.

God saved my life that stormy October day. He prevented me from becoming a casualty of the storm, though made it a very close call, in order to remind me that He was present, and that He is truly in charge, and that all I needed to do was ask for help to save my life. And, to surrender myself to Him. It was my awakening moment of clarity.

And as the saying goes, "There before the Grace of God go I."

I am deeply grateful for that experience. It is one that I reflect upon quite often, and share as a spiritual subject and tool to inspire those whom I serve.

As the song says, "There can be miracles when you believe."

Amen.

Music, Numerology, And Divine Experiences

For years, while I was in an on-and-off-again relationship with Steve, I had a specific request that I would make for validation that Spirit was guiding our loving relationship, and each day it was revealed. I would ask to hear our song, "At Last" by Etta James. I would also ask for "our number," 555, to be revealed to me. Some days it was so powerful that I would feel like the Universe was screaming, "Don't worry! Everything is going to be alright!" That number, 555, is still my favorite for Spiritual connection as it means that big exciting change is on its way! Recently, my son, Matthew, was getting on a NYC train, and as he took his seat, he saw a phone number on an advertisement banner: XXX-555-5555. He sent it to me immediately and said, "Mom, I think this is meant for you!" It never ceases to amaze me that, day after day, my signs are revealed, and so clearly. I am still in awe of it all.

Although the "on again/off again" relationship with Steve ended, the spiritual signs throughout the years that we spent together were my compass. Some guided me to understanding on a spiritual level that this particular relationship was a lesson in Divine love that still today continues to be a compass in directing me as I continue to evolve on my ongoing journey.

I understand now, years later, after spending time reflecting upon the information that I have been given from Spirit, that the relationship "presented itself" at a time when I needed to learn specific spiritual lessons early in my recovery that only this union with Steve could afford me.

"Thy Will Be Done."

Align and Co-Create

Reorganize your energy. Change your inner vibration. Remain present. Hold your vision. Set your intention. Nourish it. Speak it clearly to the Universe ... and then let it go. Get out of the way. Listen for the Universe to direct you specifically, and then take action. I observe all that is surrounding me. I no longer react. I have strived for and (achieved) equanimity to the cacophony of sounds that seek to distract me. I am at peace with wherever I am.

Trust the process. Once you let go, things seem to follow a natural flow of energy and love. A peaceful "knowing" comes along with this trust that our positive thoughts and prayers are heard. Be cognizant of the frequency of the energy you put out, as you will receive that same energy back.

Remember, "Everything is energy, and that's all there is to it. Match the frequency with the reality you want, and you cannot help but get that reality. It can be no other way. This is not a philosophy. This is physics!"

Let go and trust the Universe to be your soft place to fall!

Say aloud, "Today, I set an intention to _____ . I ask my ever-loving, enlightened, guiding Spirits to wrap their loving arms around my intention as I release it to you." Then let it go. When we have a shift in perception, and awaken to the realization that when we surrender to Spirit and "wait without anxiety," we are saying, "I trust God/Spirit/ Universe to bring to me what will serve me in my highest blessings." This is a miracle!

What do you envision co-creating with the Universe?
Write down your first two "action steps forward" that you will, or
have already, executed as a co-creator. Be sure to take your time in
implementation. Do not rush to move past these steps until you feel
ready. Ask Spirit for Divine direction.

_____

_____

_____

_____

_____

_____

How well have you followed any Divine direction you have
received in taking these steps? What specific spiritual guidance
did you receive? Did you feel any hesitation at following this
Divine direction?

_____

_____

_____

_____

_____

_____

_____

What does your Spiritual communication look like? Sound like? Feel like?

_____

_____

_____

_____

_____

_____

_____

In detail, write down one example that you have experienced where you have implemented the quote from "*A Course in Miracles*":

"*Those who are certain of the outcome can afford to wait and wait without anxiety.*"

Memorialize any monumental life lessons that you have experienced during this process thus far.

_____

_____

_____

_____

_____

_____

_____

CHAPTER 6

Transformation Through Self-Care, Boundaries, And Spiritual Solutions

"You have had the power all along."

It takes a lot of work to unlearn old thought patterns and behaviors that were ingrained in our minds as precious children by adults who didn't have the tools to care for us properly. We internalized the lack of love and attention, and the deprivation of emotional and physical safety, and blamed ourselves. As adults, we may find it hard to love and to forgive ourselves, setting no boundaries, people pleasing, allowing ourselves to continue in unhealthy relationships, and desperate to feel loved.

WE CAN UNLEARN AND RELEARN.
It is absolutely possible.

Find a professional that best serves your specific needs and with whom you feel safe. Do the work. Be curious. Try every healthy practice that falls upon your path at least once. Unlimited beliefs and the willingness to take risks will open the path to an eventful journey filled with transformation and bountiful opportunities.

Part of my self-care is setting boundaries. It benefits my personal space and informs others of my expectations for what I will, and will not accept. One who lives in an ego-based mindset, or one who is "unawakened," takes my boundaries personally and is not in alignment with my journey. For me to practice self-care, I must remain in alignment only with those who respect my personal space, my boundaries, and my desires.

Boundaries are set up to act as barriers to unwelcome attitudes, unsolicited advice, unhealthy behaviors, and unwanted advances. When we step on top of the line, blurring the lines of friendship or step way over the line into another's personal space, we are displaying lack of self-control, profound disrespect, and blatant disregard for another's values, morals, and heartfelt beliefs and desires. Once is a test; twice is a life lesson.

Pay attention if it is a lesson. Healthy living begins with healthy boundaries. State them directly and clearly. Take no prisoners.

I have grown from the mindset of a young girl who sought attention and validation for all of my choices and successes, and sought to be cradled in my pain. I have grown into a grown-ass woman whose healthy choices, self-healing, and successes promote wellness. I have had the presence of mind to make it all happen through the pain, my way.

As I was re-editing this book, according to my editor's manuscript evaluation, I knew that it would be a challenge, knowing that more details of my traumatic life experiences were going to come to the surface for me. I immediately set my self-imposed wellness boundaries into place before I began within my home, my sanctuary, to create a safe space for myself.

In the moments of recall, I also reminded myself that I have unlearned all of the toxic, unhealthy behaviors that were taught to me, and modeled for me as "normal," as an impressionable child.

Deep personal truth is something you live even when you keep it to yourself. Even when nobody else is watching or listening. It is seen in each word that you speak, and every action that you take: Integrity.

Think about your childhood, or a time in your life where you faced adversity and challenges, and the story that you created in your mind about that situation. How can you mindfully steer your thoughts from living in the past moments to bringing yourself into the present moment using healthy practices? This can be your first step.

Seek to recognize your thought(s) as a response to a real-life trauma, stress, or hardship, and as a place in time that may have altered the path that you would have chosen for yourself. Reframe the experience into a present day moment. Take small steps. Use my **S.P.E.A.R.** and **S.W.I.M. into Wellness** method to guide your recovery.

IT IS NEVER TOO LATE.

You can choose right now, in the very second that you are reading this, to create a change, one little change, that will put you on the path of wellness, and begin whatever new journey you desire. It is through spiritual solutions and daily self-care practices, with a renewed commitment, and with patience and faith, that you can access all that you desire.

It is always a choice.

S.P.E.A.R. and S.W.I.M. Into Wellness!

When you feel triggered, or you feel your symptoms escalating, **S.P.E.A.R.** first.

This is a non-linear recovery plan that is specific to your health and wellness goals.

STOP where you are.

PAUSE TO BE PRESENT. Take one slow deep breath through your nose, and exhale slowly through your mouth. Repeat three times. Your breath is your most accessible tool to intervene with your physiology in real time. Focus on your breath to align with the present moment.

EMOTE safely anything that you are feeling. You are allowed to feel whatever you feel!

Try the Alternate Nostril Breathing below to self soothe as you release your feelings/emotions.

https://www.harmonioushealth4life.com/relaxation-through-alternatenostril-breathing-wendy-blanchard-m-s-chhc/

ACCEPT your emotions and feelings. Take as long as you need to practice acceptance and validate what you are feeling in a safe space without self judgement. Acceptance promotes peace.

REST and **RE-ALIGN**, and allow yourself time to process. Hydrate! Write about it! Use the Gong Bath Meditation below as you practice Alternate Nostril Breathing, if you choose, and use my Detox Bath Recipe below to rid all of the toxins from your body. Take your time with this step. Then, **RE-FRAME** using a healthy mindset and being open to new perspectives to re-frame the experience as you move forward.

Set a **S.W.I.M. Wellness Recovery Plan** into place to be used at a glance.

Refer to your plan to bring yourself into wellness. This plan is your personal written reminder to be used at any time you begin to feel unwell, and to support you daily on your wellness journey.

This is YOUR recovery plan.

For Gong Bath video and Detox Bath Recipe, visit www.harmonioushealth4life.com.

Now…S.W.I.M. Into Wellness!

This is a non-linear recovery plan that is specific to your health and wellness goals.

Speak your truth to a trusted person. This is where your freedom begins!

What do you need in this moment/situation to provide yourself with wellness and peace? **Who** can assist you with meeting this need?

(Implement an) Integrative Approach, whatever this means for you using the body, mind and spirit wellness approach. (See examples below).

Make a Daily commitment. Create a recovery wellness plan with a professional. This could be a counselor, coach, PEER. Also share with a loved one, trusted friend, or accountability partner for support in your recovery.

Research shows us that when we practice a new healthy habit at the same time each day, we create a new healthy lifestyle change.

Examples:

Speak: I am living with an addiction/Substance Use Disorder, to drugs and alcohol, food, sex, shopping. (Truthful and authentic)

What do I need/Who is someone I trust that may be able to guide me? (I need to meet with a counselor. I need to go to treatment. I need a mindful practice to help me through this situation. I need a 12 step program. I need a crisis intervention. I need an accountability partner. I need to create a healthy lifestyle plan.)

Implement an Integrative Approach will include: (Examples):

Body: sleep, rest, short walks, exercise, mindful breathing, healthy food, water.

Mind: a support group/coach/peer/accountability partner, meditation/mindfulness/yoga, music, writing, essential oils, therapy, medication.

Spirit: prayer, nature walks, meditation, quiet time.

I suggest to commit to one small change/wellness routine at a time. For example, take a short walk, (Body), listen to your favorite music, (Mind), Try a 5 minute meditation (Spirit), daily, at the same time each day. Begin with a 30 minute self care/wellness routine. Stick with this routine for 66 days (see Make a Daily Commitment below), using the same self care tools every day. You can always practice your tools for longer periods, or shorter periods, according to your needs.

Make a Daily Commitment. Affirm: "I am committing to my wellness. As I implement my healthy lifestyle plan, I will practice the tools that resonate with me for at least 66 days at the same time each day to create structure for myself. I will continue to practice, ongoing, to achieve harmonious health for life!"

Guidance On Boundaries, Self Regulation, Healthy Practices, and Spirituality

Affirm if this resonates: "Today, I choose to let go of everything that has been toxic and causing my health and wellness to be jeopardized, and that which no longer serves me. All of it. I am practicing the self-care and self-love that I deserve."

Not too long after a day of deep meditation and prayer, and honest conversation with a mind and spiritual coach, Brett, I am ready to let it all go for me. She offered me additional tools I could use in my search for a deeper spiritual practice, and to awaken me beyond my physical limitations. Brett channels a specific message for me, "Clean up the energetic junk. Make room for all of the blessings on their way."

Amen.

When faced with adversity and challenge, we have a choice: Do we make a comeback, or do we allow a setback? Mindfully choose to make your setback become your comeback.

We empower ourselves when we go within. Our body, mind and spirit will always offer insight as to what we need in order to move forward in health and wellness. Our resilience allows us to land on our feet as we challenge ourselves, and we stretch the mind to build its strength.

Pick yourself up and dust yourself off. Clear your path to begin again. Build your resilience, learn, grow, and evolve with mindful steps. Allow yourself room to stumble and to see the view from all vantage points. Whether you are down on the ground (What do you see? What have you learned?), or steady on your feet along your path, or towering over the "junk" that you have been able to kick out of your way and off of your path once and for all, you are building resilience.

I suggest the same to you as Brett channeled for me: "Clean up the energetic junk to make room for your blessings on their way."

You cannot yell at a seed to force it to grow quickly. Instead, you love and nurture it. You meet all of its needs, and slowly, deliberately, it blooms into a beautiful flower. Find peace within yourself. Continue to stay grounded in faith, emulate gratitude, and practice patience. Go to a place of acceptance, and everything you desire will be waiting for you there.

Self-reflection is essential for one to continue to evolve. At the end of each day, assess your experiences, and forgive yourself for any perceived shortcomings, without any judgement of your actions or thoughts. Begin again with the new day that greets you, and use yesterday's experiences to create your desired outcomes. It does not matter how many mistakes we make. It is about being mindful of the lessons and opportunities we are blessed with, which allow us to grow and to evolve.

How we interpret the meaning of each experience/lesson is subjective, and very personal.

Self-awareness, through self-reflection, is a roadmap to our higher selves, where we achieve inner peace, and where we accept grace.

What is the quality of the relationship you have with yourself? How do you honor yourself daily? Write the intimate details of this relationship.

_____

_____

_____

_____

_____

_____

_____

What boundaries will you selflessly put into place as an act of self-care/self-love? Choose as many as you like, and write about it. What was the catalyst that told you it was imperative for your wellness and peace to set these boundaries? What are your new "non-negotiables"? Write it all down.

_____

_____

_____

_____

_____

_____

_____

Remind yourself every day that you have the right to set healthy boundaries in order to promote your own wellness. What are some affirmations that you can use to remind yourself that boundaries are a part of your self care?

I like to use "Post-it Notes" all around my space to visually remind me of this fact. Write them down, one on each note, and display them wherever you will see them throughout the day. ("I deserve to feel safe." I am entitled to experience peace in every moment "God/Universe/Spirit is always with me." "Boundaries keep me safe and offer me space." "I can choose a new, healthy thought right now that will promote my wellness." "I can choose to say, "No," at anytime without explaining myself.")

Create a list of at least five affirmations and/or boundaries that you would like to implement as part of your daily practice.

_____

_____

_____

_____

_____

_____

_____

_____

_____

_____

What "energetic junk" do you know that you must "clean up" to make room for your own blessings? Speak your truth!

_____

_____

_____

_____

_____

_____

What have you experienced as your most enlightening "assignments" that have allowed you to experience profound lessons and change? Write about it in detail, from the challenges to rising above the adversity. For example, saying, "No," setting healthy boundaries, leaving a toxic relationship, etc.

_____

_____

_____

_____

_____

_____

What is one truthful thought that reminds you that it is necessary for you to create change in order to experience wellness? What is one short-term goal/small action step you could set for this week that will help you to take a step towards unlearning unhealthy behaviors and/or re-learning?

_____

_____

_____

_____

_____

_____

How can you practice acceptance of your present circumstances (patience, gratitude, understanding the life lessons of the experience, having "certainty of the outcome," completely trusting your journey to God/Spirit/Universe, etc.)?

_____

_____

_____

_____

_____

_____

Write about a small yet profound lesson you experienced recently, through self-awareness and self-reflection, that provided you with the awareness needed to want to create change. How was the situation preventing you from experiencing wellness and peace?How has the Universe/God/Spirit offered guidance? How has it changed the trajectory of your journey?

In a moment when you have felt triggered, and have used my S.P.E.A.R. method, write the details of the prompting event, the details of each step you took, the how, where, when, why, and who, and how it felt when you gave yourself permission to S.P.E.A.R.

_____

_____

_____

_____

_____

_____

_____

_____

_____

_____

_____

_____

_____

Using my S.W.I.M. method, give details of your intended recovery plan. Remember that you can always modify your plan as needed. This plan is non-linear.

_____

_____

_____

_____

_____

_____

_____

_____

_____

_____

Make a copy and share it with an accountability partner.

CHAPTER 7
Strength from Within and Love All Around

"Love is always the antidote."

During these years of my recovery, I have met with many challenges. These experiences so often challenged my physical, emotional, and spiritual strength, but I was armed with many tools to assist me in navigating in a healthy way using natural and organic solutions. Perhaps the most important of these were the support system of people who helped me. This group included a professional therapist with whom I met on and off along the way, as well as Sheila, my loving friend/coach/mentor who has also counseled me from the beginning of my recovery. Others include my best friend and "sister from another mother" of thirty years, Miriam, who was my "unpaid" therapist and usually offers the best and most meaningful insight. She has been one of my greatest blessings.

In addition, my best friends of forty years, Bill and Vicky Kelder, my "brother and sister from another mother," have also always been there for me with loving insight, advice, and an empathetic ear. Bill and Vicky are the closest people that I have to family. They offer their love, friendship, and time unconditionally, and are two of my greatest blessings. We spend so much quality time together, and even after four decades of friendship, we still love being in each other's company. We have lived through so many life experiences together: the births of our children and grandchildren, marriage, illness, and even death. Our bond is forever cemented in love and friendship. Of course, my greatest and most loving Guide, is that of God/Spirit/Universe, whom I speak to daily.

I have faced losing my beloved grandmother, the one person who I knew, beyond any doubt, loved me unconditionally and with whom I had the strongest and most loving connection.

My grandmother was really my only "person." A few days after her death, I found my resiliency underneath my pain. I made a mindful choice to stay present, to ask for support from my life-transitions coach/therapist, to get outside every day (sometimes multiple times a day) for a walk, for fresh air, and to stay connected to others. I know from my own experience that isolating is extremely dangerous and unhealthy for anyone, and most especially for those of us living with substance use disorder and mental health disorders. Writing a blog and memorializing my feelings and emotions daily was cathartic, and was the catalyst (along with my spiritual practice) that brought me back to wellness. It also brought about the writing of this book.

I faced bankruptcy shortly after I began my recovery, directly following my divorce. I felt humiliated. I felt so broken and terrified of the future. What would happen to me now, with nobody but myself to rely on and no money? It was the moment to moment uncertainty that frightened me. My attorney at the time, a kind and empathetic soul, suggested that I go out and buy as many non-perishable supplies, specifically toilet paper and paper towels, as I could store in my two-bedroom condo. She said that I might not have the money to buy what I needed once bankruptcy was declared. I WAS TERRIFIED at the possibility of this becoming a reality.

It seems funny now, but I was so scared that I would not be able to afford toilet paper! I went to the supermarket and stockpiled toilet paper in order to give myself peace of mind. However, once I dug my heels in deeper to my spiritual practice, I "knew" that this type of lack would never come to pass.

Straight out of recovery, I had nowhere to live. I went to my hometown after returning from rehab in California, so I would be in familiar surroundings in Nanuet, NY. I found a motel with a tiny little kitchenette to live in for two months until I found a condo I was able to rent.

I actually began my blog back then, in July of 2013, with my son being my "editor." He kept me on a strict schedule of writing and getting the material to him within a certain number of days per week and always by midnight of those chosen days. I kept to the integrity of that schedule as the structure gave me great peace and a deep sense of predictability and accomplishment.

I would blog about my addiction recovery, as well as new recipes that I was trying that were gluten and dairy free. (I had learned during cooking classes at the rehabilitation facility that gluten and dairy were unhealthy substances.) I would take pictures of my new food creations, and post them on my website at that time along with my blogs about addiction and healthy eating for those living in recovery. My son said to me one day, after sending him one of my new blogs, "Just think, Mom, years from now, you can tell the story of how it all began again for you, and how you started this new business in a small motel room that you had to live in at the beginning of your recovery. It will be so inspiring!" He followed this up with the best piece of advice I had received in a while: "Slow and steady wins the race."

Touche.

Amen.

Slowly, I built my credit back to good standing. I prayed every single day. I remained certain, calm, and determined to succeed, always having faith in my ability and in the Universe to provide for me. Whenever I would have a fleeting thought that I might be homeless, I reminded myself that God had not brought me this far to let me fall now. I knew He had saved my life for a very high purpose. He was just providing me with the enlightening experiences that I would need to serve others. After all, it is my lived experience, and thriving recovery, that gets those I serve excited about recovery, and about working with me.

I am not a coach/counselor/consultant with only "book experience." I have lived it all, navigated it all, survived it all, and I am thriving. Most importantly, I am awakened enough to know that these lessons which I continue to experience are lifelong.

I had been living paycheck to paycheck for quite a number of years when I began my recovery, after having a life where I was financially sound and free to spend without ever looking at a price tag for anything in my twenty-four-year marriage. Clothes, jewelry, cars, trips, you name it. However, in the later years of my addiction, it was mostly my husband's earnings that provided for our family. I was too ill and drug-addicted to work or contribute regularly to our financial health.

I was being "awakened" in many areas, and shown options as I began my new solo life. These were "sobering" experiences. No pun intended. Throughout my recovery, I sometimes had as little as $30 left at the end of the month. I had no savings, and worried every day about how I would pay my bills and what I would do if an emergency should present itself. Yet, I got up every day, went to work, and showed up fully present. I did a wonderful job as I served my community as a mental health professional, Recovery Specialist, mental health community educator, and the Client/Family Advocate in mental health and substance use disorder for our county.

Very recently, after years of hard work, diligence, discipline, and determination, I found a new job that affords me financial stability. It has given me a little bit more freedom to have that weekly dinner out, or to buy a new shirt. In addition, my business as a mental health and wellness coach/consultant/educator has begun to grow. I am now being asked to do podcasts and to speak on radio shows, globally, to share my message.

During the very challenging times, I would become extremely anxious and sometimes very sad, crying every day, frustrated and angry at myself, yet I prayed for solutions and never gave up. Truthfully, I knew that I was doing the best I could, and that these circumstances were residual from my unhealthy lifestyle during my addiction. I knew that it was, in fact, just temporary. I never thought about ending my life as I had during my active addiction, and I never, ever thought about using drugs to self-medicate. Just spiritual solutions and self-care. I was, and still am, learning as I go along. The more I learn, the more I learn.

I faced a re-diagnosis of Lupus after being in remission for six and a half years, as well as a serious spine/back/leg injury that culminated in my being unable to walk, sit, stand, or lay down without pain. I had to modify my lifestyle. However, I had a feeling that much of the deeply repressed trauma and current stressors were adding to my physical pain. The body/

mind connection is so powerful. I became so tired of autoimmune flares and prayed for Spirit to show me how to heal, and to send me an authentic healer who would guide me safely, and strategically, and would offer me a long-term solution. I was being bounced around from one specialist to another, with no long-term wellness results. As the Universe always provides for me—and for you if you are open to Divine communication—I happened to be on my Instagram feed, and the first post was for a free evaluation with a business called "Phoenix Physio," which happened to be in the county where I am from. I was lying in bed in so much pain. This pain, which had been going on for weeks, occurred every couple of months. My entire body was swollen with inflammation, and I was unable to walk without pain or use my hands/wrists due to severe swelling.

I decided to click on the "Bio" of this post to see what it was all about. I was desperate for a new perspective. Dr. Zazu, Cioce, DPT, SFMA, CAPP-OB, offered an alternative type of healing that was married to traditional medicine. We immediately clicked. She listened. She heard me. She encouraged me. And after listening to my story, my concerns, and my challenges, she felt "One hundred percent" certain that she could help me to heal on a cellular level.

Wow.

Today, I continue to work with Zazu. She treats the body, mind, and spirit simultaneously, and specializes in supporting the immune system. She speaks my language. Zazu tells me that, if I do the work (You know I do it!), I will not only heal but also rid my body, once and for all, of disease and challenges and steer the trajectory of my mind and spirit to a higher level of wellness. Knowing that I will heal "one hundred percent" promotes my wellness on a cellular level. She told me that I would be able to dance again, and I did on Labor Day Weekend, 2021, while out enjoying the weekend with my dear friends, Jason and Annie. It was magical! My body was freed, and moved in ways that it hadn't moved in many years.

Zazu is one of my many earth angels. I know for certain that guiding angels heard my prayer, and guided me to Zazu.

And in addition, it is all about my mindset. I choose to be well and to do the work.

In addition, 2020-2021 has brought me new revelations about my own mental health following the death of my mother in March, 2020. When my mother died, right at the onset of lockdown due to COVID 19, I was in total shock. My mother is dead? How can that be? She was perfectly fine seven months ago!

My brain simply shut down. The "shelter in place" order due to COVID added to that stress. Now I would be working from home, (I am a Reading Specialist by day) and for me this meant quickly learning how to teach my students to read virtually when I was next to computer illiterate. (Google classroom? Camera? Chat Room? Create slides?) It also meant continuing to support my adult children, one of whom was experiencing severe anxiety daily. It was vital that I stay as connected as possible via phone, text, and FaceTime with my family and friends, for myself as well as for them, as well as with my clients. It was sometimes taxing. I did take time each day for a walk outdoors, ate healthy foods, stayed hydrated, wrote my blog, listened to my music, prayed/meditated daily, and showed up for work with great pride and willingness to do an excellent and effective job for everyone.

However, I never stopped long enough to let it soak in … to process the fact that my mother was dead. In addition, my five-year, on-again-off-again relationship with the love of my life, Steve, had come to an abrupt end. This realization was also devastating.

I began to notice, around the one-year mark of my mother's death that my anxiety was becoming harder to tame. Despite practicing all of my holistic tools, and having occasional therapy sessions with a friend/life coach, I was experiencing severe anxiety, heart palpitations, widespread body pain and swelling, constant racing thoughts, paralyzing fear, and disbelief, sleeplessness, and deep sadness with bouts of heavy sobbing that "came out of nowhere." I recognized these symptoms as a trauma response. A trauma response is "an emotional response to a deeply distressing or disturbing event." I needed to return to weekly therapy and called my former therapist, Mignyetta, for an appointment. It had been about a year since I had been working in traditional therapy. She and my life coach/friend Sheila, had both helped me greatly throughout my mother's illness, and through the first weeks after her death. I was so "together" during that time that my son even thanked me for "being so strong for everyone." I guess I was just in shock. The aftershocks came in waves, on and off, for a year after my mom died. It turns out that there was plenty of devastation within. I needed to talk, journal ... whatever it was going to take to heal. For me, this means using spiritual solutions and self care practices.

The moment that I made that appointment with Mignyetta, I felt my entire body go limp. I relaxed. I cried with gratitude and hope. Most of the body pain subsided. I felt a great sense of relief. Intuitively, I had known for quite some time that I needed to talk through my grief, but fear held me back. Acceptance of the reality of my mother's death held me back. As usual, I felt frightened about being forced to face my truth in therapy: I was deeply sorrowful over the loss of my mother. I am doing so well in therapy now, at a slow pace. As my son said, "Slow and steady wins the race."

I am tuned into all that I need, when I need it, and when I need to stop. Self awareness. Self regulation.

Mignyetta pointed out exactly what I inherently knew: I had no time or willingness to grieve my mother's death. I was in denial. I was experiencing a delayed trauma response. My mother and I had a lifelong tumultuous relationship, which was left with many loose ends because of her sudden death. Where could I fit all of that emotion? Deep, deep down in my cellular structure affecting my overall wellness. Recently, Mignyetta looked at me and said, with a huge smile and encouragement, "You are really doing the hard work!" That was so validating. It feels so amazing to feel well, physically and mentally, and I want to "live to be a hundred and twenty," as my grandmother used to say! I want to travel and speak around the world about my recovery journey to offer hope, inspiration, and suggestions through my "Wellness Approach to Recovery."

Steve and I also had a great deal of unfinished business, so Mignyetta suggested that I begin journaling through writing letters to both my mother and to Steve. This practice began my latest healing journey. "Expressive writing" and other strategies like this, where I specifically address the issues and topics that have been causing me great stress, help me to release this trauma response. It took so much courage for me to begin, but through tapping into my superpower, my courage, and my spirituality, I set out on a new healing journey.

As I journaled, I recalled that I observed unbelievable sights, sounds, and conversations during the seven months that my mother was dying. It was my first experience with witnessing one in the process of slowly dying. Her doctor told me that he had "never seen a patient so hell bent on dying." She was given a 100 percent chance of recovery, but in my mother's mind, her life was over, and she chose not to live. She refused all food, medication, and water, and ultimately died an unnecessary death. She would scream out that she wanted to die, and did not believe her doctors' evaluation that she would fully recover. She'd had an ileostomy and became fixated on "the bag," and how she could not take care of it. More accurately, she was unwilling to care for herself. She wanted someone else to care for her, and the bag. Although it was reversible, my mother was traumatized by all of it. Absolutely heartbreaking. Earlier, in 2014, when my beloved grandmother passed away, she had begun a further mental health decline. Over the years, my mother would speak unhealthy thoughts aloud, and I encouraged her to talk to someone, to no avail. Eventually, the perfect storm of bowel cancer, refusal of any food, water, or medication, and a severe and rapid decline of her mental health, which my mom had struggled with her entire life, resulted in her death.

To add to my own mental health challenges at this particular time, I could not travel to be with my mother in Florida. COVID travel restrictions were in place, and I was struggling with a serious Lupus flare resulting from this chronic load of daily stress. The guilt was eating away at my body, my mind, and my spirit. I knew why I was experiencing mental health symptoms surrounding my mother's death, and inherently, I knew that I did not want to "go there." It was surreal. I could not connect to the fact that my mother was dead, and that she had chosen this outcome.

My mother did the best that she could. That is all we can ask of anyone. And as I told my sister over and over, we have to respect mom's choices: "Mom wants peace." For my mother, this meant death. Out of frustration, my sister would scream at me that what I was saying was ridiculous. But deep down, I know she understood that this was the truth. This was all too much for our hearts to bear, and deeply traumatic. I believe that

God purposefully kept me from going to Florida to be with my mother. He knows how much of a load each of us can carry. My "backpack" was filled to capacity. I had no room left for another traumatic, up close and personal, experience. It would have been the straw to break me. I had a FaceTime hour with my mother a couple of months before her death, and it drained my wellness for weeks afterward. No amount of self care could alleviate the aftermath of that experience. So, I dug my heels in even deeper into my faith which is where I draw my strength.

After Mignyetta's suggestion, I began by journaling about twice a week, only allowing myself thirty minute increments to do so. This type of writing can bring up deeply suppressed emotions, and it did, leaving me feeling raw and naked. It was emotionally and physically draining, and it left me somewhat weak after the intense and gut wrenching sobbing that it evoked.

Please do not try this type of writing without a professional on standby to guide you.

Afterwards, I would practice some type of self-care that was healing for me: I would meditate, go for a walk, do some breath work, etc. Later, I would come back to my writing to "reframe" how I would acknowledge and accept what I had discovered through my journaling, and how I would choose to navigate it all in the future now that I had purged it. I was all cleaned out...for now. When it comes up again in the future, I have an awareness of how I want to think, and how I want to respond to my emotions and feelings in a healthier way.

In this space, I found deep empathy, compassion, and love for my mother, and I have been able to find the peace that I deserve, and to energetically offer my mother the compassion that she deserves. I could not understand any of this as a child or as an unwell adolescent and adult myself. But, I totally get it now. Mental illness is in our DNA, and is exacerbated by our environment and lack of self-care, all of which were present in my life, and in my parents' lives. It is familial and generational. I believe that I have been able to break the chain using my own awareness, self regulation, trauma work, ongoing support, and most definitely my spiritual solutions and self-care practices. Whenever I begin to feel the anxiety creep in, I go back to read my "reframing" of the experiences written in my journal, and I implement more extensive self care practices and spiritual solutions to support any dys-regulation that I may be experiencing. I have discovered forgiveness of my parents who just did not have the tools or awareness that I have been blessed to be given and to experience, as well as my deep faith.

I do the same when I do my expressive writing to Steve. I surrender it all. It is a part of my past. I mindfully choose not to bring it into my present or project it into my future. As *A Course In Miracles* states, "I can choose peace rather than this." And I do. In that peace, I am able to connect with my feelings of love and acceptance toward my parents , Steve, and for myself.

I have faced the loss of other relationships, which I decided to exit, realizing the toxicity these relationships were infusing into my life. I made a conscious decision to cut out anyone from my life who could not respect my boundaries, and/or consistently made unreasonable demands on my time and on my energy. I began to feel so exhausted and so unwell due to these relationships. We know that toxic relationships cause inflammation on a cellular level. I lived with inflammation due to these types of relationships for decades. "I choose peace rather than this."

One family member in particular would call me every day, hysterical. The calls were manipulative in nature, with threats of suicide being used as a bargaining tool. I called for help for this family member multiple times over a matter of months, but she always fell back into a manipulative pattern. She would continue to bully me for what she wanted, and even refusing to speak to me, something I was very accustomed to with her throughout my life. When that didn't work, I'd get the cold shoulder for weeks at a time. This is a specific type of mental abuse. I had been abused with this tactic for decades.

Now, I had set boundaries in place. I had to detach.

It is my wellness that must be my first priority. If I don't make it my first priority, who will? I depend solely on myself to experience daily wellness and peace. I always say, "If anything or anyone disturbs my peace ongoing, I make a mindful decision to divorce them from my space, and from my life. No ill will on my part. This is my self-care." And, I cannot care for another who does not care for themselves, and certainly not more than they care for themselves.

I do not live in fear of losing others from my life. The only thing I fear is losing myself to the agendas of other people that do not serve my best interest. I never second guess the steps that I take. I walk with our Creator.

I am an excellent student, and He is an excellent teacher.

Suggestions To Tap into Your Inner Strength Through Spiritual Solutions

You have no idea what you are made of until the candle burns out and you are left to use that tiny little ember to ignite the flame that will light your way. It's that or "rest in pieces" in the hollow, dark hole. Challenge yourself. When you finally rise up, a little bruised but not broken, you will begin to live. My greatest spiritual shifts have come through the willingness to "take my own inventory" as is stated in the twelve-step community. It always turns out that the anticipation of taking the action is what I fear, but I do it anyway. Afterwards, I reflect on what I was in fear of, and realize that it was of not being perfect. Now, whether I succeed or whether I need to try again, I have successfully and willingly taken a risk, which builds my self confidence, experiences, and resiliency. The more we practice resiliency, the more we build resiliency. There is a saying in the "twelve-step" community that I love: "You are only as sick as your secrets."

LIVE – YOUR – TRUTH. SPEAK – YOUR – TRUTH.

In the quiet of our space, we have the awareness of what our truth really is. This is where freedom begins.

What adversity and/or challenges have you experienced that has encouraged you to tap into your inner strength, and that of Spirit, to promote your own wellness and peace?

_____

_____

_____

_____

_____

_____

_____

What truth have you spoken to initiate your first step towards wellness and change?

_____

_____

_____

_____

_____

_____

_____

What have you learned about your own resiliency?

_____

_____

_____

_____

_____

_____

_____

How have these experiences enhanced your journey? What was
the gift/gifts in these experiences? What is your re-frame of this
experience moving forwards?

_____

_____

_____

_____

_____

_____

_____

_____

CHAPTER 8
Fearless, Faith, And Freedom

"Never let your fear decide your future."

Until I sought help to arrest my addiction and to treat my mental health disorders, I lived every day in fear of everything. This kept me in a chronic state of anxiety (a heightened sense of nervous awareness of others and of my surroundings): racing heart, racing thoughts, numbness and tightness throughout my body, headaches, nausea, diarrhea, irritability, etc. I took an exorbitant amount of Xanax to try to calm my anxiety and fear. I believe that the amount I was ingesting, along with the opiates, exacerbated my anxiety.

I feared making the wrong choices, the wrong decisions, and not getting the approval of others. I lived for praise as a compass for how well I was doing, and how much I was liked and loved.

I lived in a "what if" mindset. "What if I make a mistake? What if they don't like me? What if I fail at trying something outside of my comfort zone? What if they get mad at me?" These questions prevented me from evolving. My fear paralyzed me from taking any risks or chances that could have given me opportunities to grow and to learn. I could not identify who I was, because I lived in the shadows of who others said I "should" be. Have you ever heard the saying, "Don't 'should' all over yourself?" *Touché.*

Once I went into recovery and began to heal, I realized that I am the only person I am responsible for, and I cannot control what others may think, how they may behave, or if they will approve of my choices. It's not my business. That is their crap. Whatever *they* think about me is about them. When others are judging us, they are seeing themselves in the mirror that we hold up to them, revealing their own reflection. It is in that mirror that one sees their own truth. They make a decision to either create change, or back away in fear, living in a false sense of security. Sometimes another may *want* what we have, but they live in fear of being uncomfortable. So, when they see themselves in us, it may be a trigger for them. Will they step up, or step away?

Straight out of recovery, I had been working with my life coach, Maria. I felt, at that time, that Maria was supporting me tremendously, and that I did not need traditional therapy. And for that specific time in my life, it worked. Subsequently, I began traditional therapy in conjunction with my work with Maria.

I now have the experience of discernment. I will no longer "consciously" shovel the dirt from the past into my present-day living. I understand that I can be, and will be, triggered at times, but that discernment is my friend. I have also learned, many years later in my wellness, that we can have deep remnants of trauma suppressed very deep within our cellular structure. We may not even know it until something profound triggers us and we "re-experience" the emotions and feelings as if it were the original trauma. Each time the trauma response rears its ugly, yet meaningful, place in my awareness, I begin a new awakening, and a new healing journey. This time from experience, and armed with more tools and a deeper awareness than I had at the onset of my recovery journey.

I wanted to understand my addiction, empathize with it, make peace with it, release the trauma through self-discovery, and get well so that I could live my best life. I had not lived yet. I began to heal my trauma through talk therapy and my willingness to try a multitude of natural and organic solutions as I began a holistic health lifestyle right out of treatment in early 2013. This was a huge part of my awakening, and where I was set free.

My greatest fear was setting boundaries with anyone. I used to be a people pleaser, and would never say no. I feared that others would get mad at me, or no longer like me or want to spend time with me or be my friend. Even with family members, who were clearly disrespecting my kindness and my willingness to help, I would continuously allow their behavior to control me. I would find myself enveloped in their unhealthy web of dysfunction. I allowed it to continue because I felt that, the more I did so, the more I would be loved. *On my wellness journey, I have been enlightened.* The truth is, the more I did for others that went unappreciated and unnoticed, the more drained and exhausted and resentful I felt. And none of it enhanced my own life. There was rarely ever any reciprocity or gratitude. The more I did, the more I was asked to do, and expected to do, with more frequent and irrational demands on my time and energy.

I began to set healthy and firm boundaries and would say no whenever I felt I would be overextending myself or whenever I felt that whatever was being asked would not serve me. And, I do not explain my answer. I do not begin with the words, "I'm sorry, but I can't help you." It is simply, "No. I cannot do that." I will no longer go into "debt" energetically for anyone else at the expense of my own wellness.

I practice self-care first. If something that I am being asked to do is going to jeopardize my wellness, or expend and deplete my energy, the answer is "no." No regrets. No apologies. Those who are coming from a good and loving place support and respect my boundaries. If they do not support my boundaries, they are not meant to be aligned on my path.

About one year ago, an immediate family member called me, whom I love dearly, yet again, for help. This individual has been living with mental illness and substance use disorder for about twenty years. Her path has been very similar to my own, so my empathy and compassion runs deep. She had been in and out of treatment for both SUD and mental illness for years, but always refused the long term, intensive treatment that she needed to heal. It began to take a toll on my physical and mental health. My wellness was being compromised. Steve had always told me that I should "love her from afar," yet I felt a responsibility for her wellness. Until it began to deplete mine.

This last event was eye opening. She was clearly experiencing severe symptoms of mental illness, and admitted to me that she was using drugs daily. Because she had, many times previously, been suicidal, and in fact, attempted suicide, I called for help for her. I am trained to know when I can help, and when it is beyond my scope of training.

By the time I arrived, along with the professionals in our county, to administer aid, she was escalated in her symptoms, and once she saw me, she began giving me the middle finger with both hands and screaming, "I hate you! Get off my property!" I guess I had become numb to these outbursts, because I walked up to the police who were there with the local mental health emergency mobile unit and said, "I'm going home. I know she is in good hands." I turned my back, got into my car, and drove home, about forty minutes away. In the meantime, my son got a message about all of this and called me to beg me not to "get sick over this." I assured my son that I was fine and wasn't taking this personally as I knew that this individual was deeply unwell.

I arrived home and allowed myself to feel it all: her pain, my empathy for her, and the loss of this relationship that I finally had to admit was over, for now. I was sobbing so hard and so excessively that I felt faint. My heart was beating in a way I had never felt before. I felt like vomiting. My left arm felt numb and tight, and my face as well. I calmed myself through breath work, and then called a therapist friend to talk it out. Although I knew I was doing the best thing for myself, and that she was being well taken care of, and that the Universe was guiding me in this way, part of me knew that this was going to take a great deal of discipline. No more contact. It was too lethal. I deserve to live my life in peace, and to be well. I will never forget how the police were holding her back. It took two of them to hold back a one-hundred-pound woman. The look in her eyes was terrifying. I did not know who I was looking at. She was a stranger. A prisoner being held hostage by her own mind.

I refuse to place myself in any situation that is so toxic and unhealthy. You see, a great deal of my faith also comes from realizing that my recovery must be my utmost priority. I will never allow another human being, no matter who they are, to jeopardize my wellness, or my recovery. I have done my work, and continue to do so, fearlessly. If someone else continues to infuse me with their toxicity, I have the tools to say, "No." No matter what. No matter who it is.

"No."

My wellness is my responsibility and my priority. In the future, if she is able and willing to seriously seek the help that she needs, I will guide her. But nothing more. We must choose to be pro-active in our wellness, and in our evolution.

That's it.

This was my fearless faith offering me freedom. It was a choice that I had to make. A no brainer. I no longer take anything personally. I remind myself that any unkind words or actions that another person takes and flings in my direction is about them. I have the choice to walk around the muck, and cross the street. The beautiful soul underneath this mental illness did not have the awareness to recognize that she was so unwell. We cannot force another person into wellness.

I stand firmly in my own wellness. I use my tools. I stand deeply in my faith. And I am fearless in securing my joy, my peace, and my serenity through my deep faith and connection to Spirit.

This past year has gotten a little easier. I pray for her and for her family every morning and every night before I close my eyes. I have a "knowing" that God has His loving arms wrapped around her, and her sweet family. He doesn't need my help. And if, at some point, He needs me to "work" on His behalf, I will "know."

In the past, I would've been too afraid to walk away, with the "what ifs" plaguing me. "What if she dies?" "What if they take her to the hospital?" "What if she hates me because I've called for help?" "What if she over-doses again, and I'm not there with my Narcan kit?"

A couple of years ago, I had run to her aid with my Narcan kit after she didn't answer her phone for twenty-four hours. I finally heard from her when I left a message saying that I was bringing the police if I didn't hear from her within fifteen minutes. I hadn't slept or eaten. My IBS was out of control as I sat on the toilet with diarrhea for hours, and then needing an over-the-counter anti-diarrheal drug to even be able to leave my home. I finally heard from her. She was in a complete drug-induced state. I went to bed.

This had to stop.

The truth is that I had expected the reaction that I got this last time. And I was prepared for it. I knew that what I was doing was what was best for her, and for her family, and I have no regrets.

It is always in the back of my mind that she *could* die. From the drugs. From a completed suicide. From a heart attack brought on by years of a serious and profound eating disorder, or a combination. *Yes, exactly my old story.* However, I have mindfully changed my narrative with years of discipline, eagerness to experience wellness, and hard work. I am very secure in my own wellness, physically, mentally, and spiritually. As such, I know that, if that should happen, it has absolutely nothing to do with me or with anything that I did, or did not do. And I am at peace with it all. Most of the time. I pray for His strength daily. I pray for His loving arms to be wrapped around her, protecting her at all times. I pray. I pray. I pray.

Fearlessness. Faith. Freedom. Knowing that God/Spirit/Universe has got it covered allows me to be free.

"There before the Grace of God go I."

Inspiration for Practicing Fearlessness

When we retreat and just accept what is, without taking chances on what more we can accomplish or achieve, we remain stuck. We often tend to play it small, as this feels safer in the comfort zone we have created. As we follow the strong sensation of being pulled outside of the box that we've remained in for too long, we begin to experience the palpable rush of our true desires. We begin to evolve as we allow ourselves to be free to explore the infinite possibilities of the Universe.

It is the anticipation of the act that we fear. When we find our courage, our voice within, our own intuition, divinely led, we are guided, to step out of our comfort zone. We burst out of our chrysalis and we fly.

Being willing to do the hard work that offers us opportunities to learn and to evolve is a deliberate path to a spiritual awakening.

Fear leads us to false perception. *It is not real.* It is based upon our past experiences that we continue to hold on to, and sometimes it is even buried deeply within our cellular memory. In order for our present circumstances to turn out differently, we must have an awareness, be open to other perspectives, believe that change is possible, and follow Spirit's guidance.

People do change, and things can change, once we correct the negative thinking that keeps us stuck in a fearful mindset. Once we believe that change is a possibility, and we come from a mindset of love for ourselves and empathy for all that we have endured, we immediately make a shift from feelings of fear to an abundance of love.

When I am faced with a harsh reality that brings fear, I feel like I want to run as far and as fast as my legs will take me to avoid the pain of a situation I do not want to face. Instead, I breathe into it slowly, deeply, and steadily. I observe the feeling, and I do not give in. I acknowledge the feeling, and then I choose, mindfully, in that moment, *a response that is the opposite of fear.* I keep myself engaged calmly, confidently, and constructively, one moment at a time. I allow myself the space to grow and find resolve, rather than hiding from the truth, however painful.

The truth is always calm. Untruths are a cacophony of noises trying to mask the calm for fear of the truth. That is when we must face ourselves, if we are brave. Here is where our awakening begins.

Feeling a strong emotion that suddenly triggers a response, such as fear, is our invitation to feel it all the way through, sit with it, process it for as long as it takes, and release it when we feel we are ready (and not a moment before). Use it for enlightenment, healing, and moving forward. Reframe. This is how we uncover the fear that we don't realize is deep within. It is a spiritual call for change. Recognize the feeling in the moment and identify it. This is an opportunity to deepen our faith, to experience freedom, and to *be fearless in experiencing our experiences.*

Fear is an unhealthy habit. The secret to breaking this habit is a four-letter word: L.O.V.E.

Letting Our Vulnerability Emerge!

Here is where we become completely naked with absolutely no apologies for how we present.

Vulnerability is born on a spiritual path where you are certain you are supported, guided, and loved by the Universe. This heightens your faith in feeling free to divorce from the ego, which fuels fear. Extinguish the ego with L.O.V.E. for Ego is not connected to Spirit. Show ego the way to love.

What are you afraid of? What are your top-two greatest fears?
What, or whom, are you afraid of losing if you simply say, "no"? Write
about it.

_____

_____

_____

_____

_____

_____

When you finish, pause. Find compassion for the feelings that you
have just allowed yourself to experience. Honor your feelings.
Emotions need motion to move through us, so allow them to
move through you as you walk, dance, exercise, etc., all the while
being present with those feelings. Allow yourself as much time as
you need.

_____

_____

_____

_____

_____

_____

Take some time for a meditation, walk, or any type of self care when you have completed writing. When you feel ready, reflect on your writing. No self judgement. What self care practice did you implement? Were you able to stay in the "no judgement zone" after your reflection of what you have written? What did that feel like? Write it all down.

_____

_____

_____

_____

_____

_____

_____

_____

Lastly, write with a reframe by validating what you have discovered, what you are feeling, and how you will make a choice to use this information. Your re-frame will be positive and constructive. It will no longer fuel your fear moving forward.

_____

_____

_____

_____

_____

Write down two affirmations that you may say to yourself when you feel your fear escalating. ("I am in control of my thoughts," or "I choose not to allow myself to give into my fear. I choose, instead, to breathe, to not react, and to take the opposite action of what I know has not worked for me in the past." "I choose a 'time out'." "I can choose peace rather than this." "Fear is just a feeling.")

_____

_____

_____

_____

_____

_____

_____

_____

_____

_____

_____

_____

_____

_____

_____

Write down two action steps that you can immediately implement as part of your self-care to de-escalate your feelings of fear. This could be deep breathing, writing, prayer, meditation, a change of your activity or environment, calling someone you trust to talk it out or just to be heard, taking a walk, and/or simply saying "No" to whatever it is that is causing your symptoms to escalate. And you may implement my S.P.E.A.R. steps when your feelings feel escalated. You are NOT your feelings.

Ask yourself these questions:

"What is the worst that could happen if I do not try to control the outcome of this situation?"

"What action would serve me best in this moment?"

"What could I say "No" to that would alleviate my anxiety and offer me peace? "What could I say "Yes" to that would enhance my wellness?"

"What do I need in this moment, or in this situation, to provide me with peace/wellness? How can I move towards that goal? Go back to the S.W.I.M. method in Chapter 6 to re-read, edit, add, or begin again to implement the steps of this program through your own awareness.

Begin writing it all down here:

_____

_____

_____

_____

_____

_____

_____

_____

_____

Remember, you have the right to experience peace and wellness in every moment, and you are the only person who can provide that for yourself.

CHAPTER 9
Intentional Wellness

Intentions are a positive way to start and help focus my day. Each day after my prayer and meditation practice, I set an achievable intention that will serve me throughout the day. This offers me a preconceived awareness of how I want my day to unfold that aligns with my highest self and how I want to react with others. I may set an intention as simple as, "I will smile at everyone today," or "Today I will use adversity as my teacher!" Often, I use intentions that are simple, but some days when I am feeling really brave, I set an intention that is somewhat challenging! (Yes, challenge yourself!) One of my more taxing intentions, "I will see myself in everyone today, no matter how negatively or unkindly others may behave toward me." "I will be the light," sometimes requires that I remind myself of my intention many times throughout the day, even within a single hour, sometimes even within minutes of my original self-reminder.

On challenging days, I sometimes begin to feel fear creeping in or my anxiety beginning to escalate. At these times, I repeat my intention silently to myself and use a simple deep-breathing technique. This technique, known as "Alternate Nostril Breathing," is a Pranayama practice that is extremely helpful in de-escalating anxiety. (Find the steps to this breathing technique on my website.). Box breathing is also a helpful tool for de-escalation. First, breathe in deeply through the nose for four seconds, Then, hold your breath for four seconds, and finally, breathe out through your mouth for four seconds. After completing these practices, I quickly feel realigned with my wellness. Even when intentions or situations can be challenging, having the awareness of what I need is validating. Taking a moment to check in with myself through self-awareness and breathing is all part of self-care. This is time well-spent!

I also state the intentions of my desired manifestations.

In 2019, through writing and in prayer, I began setting the intention of finding a new job where I could work with youth who needed my expertise in social/emotional learning (SEL) in order for them to feel heard and validated.

It was also my intention to earn more money so that I could support myself more effectively. I began each day by asking the Universe to guide me to my desire, and in the meantime at my current job, the Universe provided me with constant opportunities to practice teaching my "social emotional learning" presentations and curriculum, along with my mental health and wellness trainings. I was being called by our school districts, local colleges, and teacher's center to provide my trainings to staff and to students, as well as "family universities" set up in our school districts to educate families and caregivers on mental health and wellness, including SEL. I used these opportunities to prepare myself for (the journey) the job that I was manifesting (destination), which I was certain would come to fruition. In about thirteen months, I arrived at my destination. I began teaching reading through a social emotional learning program in a district where the demographic, specifically, needed my guidance, and I was asked to teach Mental Health & Wellness, and Mental Health First Aid for Youth in our district, as well as at our teacher's center! *I NEVER GAVE UP ON MY INTENTION.*

Remember this quote? *A Course In Miracles* says, "Those who are certain of the outcome can afford to wait and wait without anxiety." I was certain of the outcome. I knew I was being diligent in my research, in furthering my education, and in creating a variety of important lessons on a topic, "Social Emotional Learning," which as I have said, is trending. I taught it so often, receiving accolades and positive feedback on my work, that I *knew* I was being groomed by the Universe for the position of my dreams. *Through intention, we manifest. Through unwavering faith and gratitude, we arrive at our desired outcome.* Recently, I created a training workshop for educators and support staff, entitled, "Mental Health and Wellness Literacy," and piloted it to rave reviews! I am now offering this training worldwide, and receiving rave reviews. I am busy filling up my schedule! In this time of COVID 19, it is even more important that our school communities be empowered through educational workshops that offer information on mental health and wellness. My trainings also promote understanding of how trauma may be underlying brain disorders that affect one's mental health. In addition, I have gone on to create a myriad of other professional development trainings also to rave reviews! Through all of this hard work, my business is growing, and I am able to earn more money to support myself comfortably.

"Intention initiates indescribable innovation!": I stated my intention, stood fearlessly in my faith, worked hard, researched, practiced, and never gave up. I trusted that it would come to fruition through Divine communication, and today, I am living my dream!

I am in beautiful alignment with the Universe/God/Spirit. I experience serendipitous synchronicities throughout each and every day. I have a clear understanding of my spiritual connection, and I know exactly when I am being "spoken to" by the Universe. I receive signs and messages that are so clear in their content and intent. If we are open to Spiritual communication, and follow this Divine direction, we will receive the most meaningful and unconditional love and support far beyond any other we could have imagined being connected to. We will have information and direction that will help us to achieve our highest blessings.

But … we must do the work. And, we must be a humble student with the willingness to see new perspectives through the eyes of the Divine.

As I write and edit this book, I receive "downloads" from the Universe. I smile, shake my head in awe, and blow kisses with my hands, looking up at the sky in awe and gratitude. The words are being channeled from Spirit to me and onto the computer. Spirit is guiding me in writing and editing! It is so amazing! State your intentions, believe, and receive!

Proceed with your day feeling assured that all has been heard and, if it will enhance your life, it will be brought to you in the right time. Practice patience and faith. Always know and believe in the power of prayer and gratitude. Each day, write down your intention, say it aloud, give thanks, and release it into the Universe. Trust. Believe. Memorialize each step as you watch it unfold. You will experience a miracle in the right place at the right time. *With faith, hope, and love, anything is possible!*

Letting go of the tight grip has freed my hands to dig in deep and play in the dirt, to explore and to experience, knowing that the beauty of the blooming buds has covered most of the weeds that were strangling my growth.

I avoid long-term resolutions as it is much easier to set and achieve short-term goals. When we are successful short-term, it motivates us to continue. So, my intention is to remain in balance at all times and strive for equanimity. I do not panic or become too excited when life deviates from the norm. I strive not to get too comfortable when the waters are calm, but rather to enjoy it in the moment, knowing its presence is a temporary gift. I am setting an intention to remain present to all that is happening around me, without putting too much emphasis on what I hope the outcome could be. I am certain that, whatever the outcome, my highest blessings are being delivered! Remember, "Those who are certain of the outcome can afford to wait, and wait without anxiety."

What is your intention today? Tell the Universe and then hold the space in your thoughts and in your heart. Believe in that intention with conviction, because wherever, and whenever we focus our intention, our energy directs and manifests. Once we share our desired intentions clearly with the Universe/God/Spirit, we co-create our miracles. As Deepak Chopra states, *"Everything that happens in the Universe starts with intention."*

Every day, record your simple desired intention, and then separately, record your intention for manifestation. Record all of the serendipitous synchronicities that you experience daily throughout your journey. Remember, it is always about the journey, so pay close attention along your path! Listen and watch beyond your physical limitations. "Tune in" to your intuition. This is where your strongest spiritual connection resides.

Include the date and time on each page. Offer gratitude after each interaction with Spirit. Throughout your journey, notice and record the specific twists and turns along your journey prior to reaching your destination. They have all been Divinely orchestrated as teachable moments by the Divine. Immerse yourself in the miracle of every Divinely directed moment. There is a life lesson in each one.

What aspect of your spiritual practice helps to strengthen your "intention" muscle?

_____

_____

_____

_____

_____

_____

_____

_____

_____

What "download" have you received from the Universe that you may use to realign when you experience uncertainty and anxiety?

_____

_____

_____

_____

_____

_____

_____

Borrowing from Gabby Bernstein's morning journaling exercise, ask yourself, "How do you want to feel today?" What is your intention to achieve that goal? Write it down."

_____

_____

_____

_____

_____

_____

_____

How do you *want* to be experienced by others today? What is your intention to achieve that goal?

_____

_____

_____

_____

_____

_____

Keep a daily journal as an everyday reminder of these intentions, placed somewhere accessible so you can receive reassurance and validation at a glance.

CHAPTER 10

Awareness of Self, Others, And Spirit

"Accepting Grace"

When we encounter conflict despite our practicing awareness of ourselves and others, it is helpful to remember these four suggestions in order to arrive at a mutually beneficial and constructive resolution:

1. Do not react.

2. Listen without judgement of others, and practice non-judgement of ourselves.

3. BREATHE. Observe your feelings and emotions. Allow them to pass through you for as long as it takes, and if warranted, take a timeout.

4. Respectfully and sincerely validate all feelings, and state a clear intention for a mutually-beneficial, and positive outcome.

Recently, I created these four steps as a way to remind myself at-a-glance how to practice spiritually aligned actions. For example, my friend and colleague, David Rahman, and I, disagreed on the initial draft of his Foreword for this book. David sent me the draft, and as a teacher, I felt there were a few places that needed to be edited for clarity of meaning. I edited the Foreword, and sent it back for David's approval. However,

David was not okay with some of the edits, as he felt that it changed the meaning of what he was trying to convey.

In an email, David sent me the draft, and as a teacher, I could see a few places that, in my opinion, needed to be edited for clarity of meaning. I edited the foreword, and sent it back for David's approval. David sent it back immediately and said that he was not okay with some of the edits, as he felt that it changed the meaning of what he was trying to convey.

Immediately, I felt old triggers sneak in. As a child and young adult, I was never heard, and my feelings had to be kept quiet. Whenever I wanted to discuss or share my feelings, I was told, "Get out of my sight, you little bastard, or I'll break your neck!" Because of this trauma, I was allowing my past experiences to bleed into this present situation, despite the fact that David had not said or done anything remotely warranting the rush of feelings that surfaced! My heart began to race, my head felt tight, and I felt hot all over. Without thinking or breathing, allowing myself the space to understand David's words, or offering validation of what he was feeling, I sent the email right back to him and said, "Then maybe we shouldn't use your foreword." I had literally fallen into a fight or flight mindset, and, in that mindset, I had hundreds of irrational thoughts swirling around in my mind. Only a few moments later, I realized they had absolutely nothing to do with the present situation.

Regressing into an old mindset (we all falter, but it's how quickly we recover that counts) was my way of trying to "be heard." Trauma leaves an emotional, behavioral, and mental imprint, so that when something feels the same as that traumatic painful experience, it activates the thought patterns linked to the initial trauma. This makes you think, act, react, and feel in the same way you did when it first happened, even though it is a different experience." David emailed back and said, "Okay, we won't use it." The moment that I read his words, I felt the "fear chills" as I call it, thinking I had done something "bad," and that my friend would not want me in his life anymore (This was based on my past experiences with my mother).

Then it was as if Spirit embraced all of me, whispered to me, and suggested that I reach out to David. I felt an immediate calm. This helped me to trust my friend and approach the situation coming from a humble, loving, and spiritually-aligned place. I texted David and asked if we could have a conversation, and he said, "Of course!" In addition to being colleagues, David and I are friends, and I admire him in his own right as a mental health educator who helps many people around the world. Before we spoke, I wanted to remind myself of the spiritually aligned action(s) that would offer an outcome we could both be excited about and that would act as a reminder to myself to remain present throughout our dialogue. I needed something tangible and structured for my own "mental reference" in order to exhibit the behavior that I wanted to present. After I calmed down, I knew that I was experiencing a spiritually directed opportunity to learn, to grow, and to evolve. The words came pouring out onto the paper. This was Divine guidance! This would become a worthwhile lesson that I could share with others, and here I am sharing it with you!

The four steps listed above came pouring onto the paper immediately. I *knew* Spirit was speaking through me, channeling, as I wrote them down and placed them in front of me for my FaceTime with David. Leading up to that call, I was in a heightened state of anxiety. My heart was racing, my hands were shaking, my legs felt weak, and I realized in that moment that this was always my reaction to my mother's explosive rages towards me: crippling fear and anxiety. Fortunately, through my years of recovery using healthy practices and mindfulness, I was able to remind myself that in the present moment, I was safe, in my own home, preparing for a healthy conversation with my good friend. This was discernment.

As I allowed David to explain why he was feeling that some of the edits were not edits he could live with, I could feel my anger/anxiety escalating. Trauma was yelling at him, *"You're not right! I'm a teacher! You don't value my input! You don't hear me!"*

Trauma is hard to tame, but not impossible.

Because I had written down the steps I wanted to follow and had it within my immediate view, I continuously looked at the words as a compass. I kept saying to myself, *"David has the right to feel how he is feeling, and I must validate his feelings as I would like my feelings to be validated."* I listened to his words while reminding myself to come back to the present as my racing thoughts popped in and out. I kept reminding myself that *"This situation is in the present, and is in no way linked to, or reflective of, my past trauma."* Even though we could see each other eye to eye, I took long, deep breaths in between his words. David knows my history well, and he was brilliant in allowing me to feel what I was feeling as we negotiated his text, never taking his eyes from mine. This was so validating and comforting. Rather than yelling, not listening to me, and storming away as I was used to, he remained present, steady, and kind with me the entire time.

He has been a gift along the way of my recovery.

We negotiated for about an hour, and the result is the eloquent and heartfelt Foreword to this book. Recognizing our trauma when it pops up without warning can help us to heal the irrational thoughts and behaviors we experience. If we are willing to use our connection to the Universe/ God/Spirit, we can create magnificent, constructive, meaningful, and permanent change, even in the face of a temporary trauma response.

Spirit will show us the way out.

My most sacred connection is with Spirit. Throughout my active addiction, I was blessed with a strong and loving connection to the Universe/ God/Spirit. So, although my mindset was altered by the pills that I was taking, I still experienced a deep awareness and connection to Spirit. It is definitely stronger and more palpable than any drug. I knew, intuitively, that I was gravely ill, and that I needed help to save my life. It was so clear to me that, the more I prayed, the more I heard and felt Spirit's presence, offering me many opportunities to ask for help. I would experience serendipitous synchronicities. I would receive "messages" and what I refer to as "signs" that would offer me solutions and reassurance that I was surrounded by loving Spirit. Now, on the other side of my addiction, living in recovery, Spirit's presence is stronger than ever before. My senses are now highly aligned with Spirit, and through daily communication, I am certain that I am in the presence of the Divine.

The morning before I asked for help, I can recall sitting on the couch in my home watching television. Spirit spoke to me through a moderator on the morning NBC newscast. I remember it so vividly, and I knew that the Universe/God/Spirit was speaking directly to me. I was completely awake, and aware of an intense Spiritual awakening happening for me in real time. The newscaster began talking about rising rates of prescription-drug addiction, and the loss of life related to addiction (also known as substance use disorder). As if speaking to me personally, he looked directly into the camera and said, "There is help available. You are not alone." I got a visceral feeling in the pit of my stomach. I knew Spirit was speaking to me through him, and I immediately began sobbing uncontrollably and saying, "Thank you," to God for this reassurance and loving guidance.

Being aware of my own truth and of my deeply rooted connection to Spirit allowed me to finally speak my truth to my primary-care physician, Dr. Bruce Levitt. He sent me to the emergency room at our local hospital, and after twenty-four hours, I was transferred to the detox and recovery unit. After five days, I left for California to visit my one hundred year old grandmother, Nanny, who had been my loving lifeline throughout my life. I thought I would rest and recover on my own terms in her home, without in-patient care or out-patient care and maybe just attend a few twelve-step meetings. In my mind, I had gone through five days of detox, so I had done what I needed to in order to heal. However, by the grace of God's profound presence, within less than forty-eight hours, I became aware of just how physically and mentally ill I was. I went through severe withdrawal for about a week. I experienced crippling flu-like symptoms, cardiac symptoms, debilitating gastrointestinal symptoms, and intense irritability. My legs felt like I had bugs crawling inside of them, and they were jerking involuntarily. I experienced delusions in which I began seeing things and hearing things that nobody else heard or saw.

I watched so much television, trying to distract myself from the symptoms of withdrawal. I could have sworn that I saw my husband on the television at the Boston Marathon, where bombs had just detonated. It was April 15, 2013, and I was convinced that he was involved in some way. I was painfully aware that I needed intensive treatment, in-patient care, and medical supervision to safely detox the rest of the way, and to begin my healing journey with the greatest chance of a full recovery, body, mind, and spirit. That old mindset of "I know what is right," and "my way is the right way," as I had used with my friend, David, now needed to be reset. I was finally ready. Despite feeling alone and scared in my mental and physical pain, I was so cognizant of my spiritual connection. I still felt loved and supported. I never felt judged. I had a distinct "knowing" that the moment I asked for this higher level of care, the Universe would guide me to it safely through Spirit. Once I actually spoke my truth out loud, asking God to "show me the way out" of this disease, I was led directly and immediately to the people who could provide me with the care that I needed. I picked up the phone and called a facility in Costa Mesa, California. One of the counselors that I worked with at the hospital during my five-day detox in N.Y. had wisely provided me with this contact information when I left the hospital, just in case I decided to ask for more intensive care in the future. This was Divine intervention lovingly guiding me, and protecting me. Even in my pain and fear of what was to come, I was aware of God's plan. All I had to do was ask, and I would be guided. I asked, and I received. When we are open to Divine communication, we will hear and see beyond our physical limitations. Here are three stories of epic awareness—awareness of self, of another, and of Spirit:

Always "Look Up Child"

In July 2021, as I sat working on Chapter One, I pondered a title for the chapter that was about overcoming the abuse and challenges of my childhood that led to addiction and my eventual turning to God/Spirit/ Universe for support and loving guidance to save my life. Nothing was coming to mind, so I got up to make some tea and said to myself, "I don't need a title just yet. I will think about it." As I began to walk towards the kitchen, Lauren Daigle's song, "*Look Up Child*," began to play. God/ Spirit/Universe always speaks to me through music, and this time was no different. I stopped right in my tracks, and turned around to look at the Bluetooth speaker, saying to myself (and then aloud), "Thank you, Spirit!" I immediately realized that *THIS* was a Spiritual suggestion for the Chapter One title! It was so awesome and so "normal" in my Spiritual connection! I am always given guidance and direction to my highest blessings! I called my son, Matthew, to share that the Universe had just communicated with me with a suggested title that was perfect! I never would have come up with that on my own!

"*Look up child, look up ...*" – sung by Lauren Daigle

This song has become a soothing self care tool. Whenever I begin to feel doubt and worry, this song almost immediately begins to play on Pandora. Energetically, Spirit sends me this "sign" to remind me to "Look up, Child. Everything is in my hands, I've got this, I've got you, and everything is going to be alright." And it always is. It is an instant re-alignment for my anxiety. Spirit is always present! Every answer that I ever need always presents itself when I "look up."

Brian Bailey – "This Little Light Of Mine."

An experience with my friend, Brian, provides a profound example of both receiving, and giving of God/Spirit/Universe's grace. Our friendship shows how at different times, each of us is guided by Spirit to Divinely support and to help others.

Recently, as I read my dear friend Brian's Instagram page about his own book being prepared for publishing, my heart filled with so much gratitude and love for my friendship with him. We met in 2013, shortly after I began my recovery, at a twelve-step meeting that I decided to try. It turned out that the twelve-step approach was not for me, and instead, I opted to create and follow my own holistic *Wellness Approach to Recovery."* However, Brian was the Divine blessing and gift in my short time of attending these meetings. Spirit brings us all that we need— people, situations, and places—in the most creative and healing ways. Brian was another "gift along the way" on my path of recovery

Brian's journey was one of severe childhood abuse and neglect. He was imprisoned and sexually trafficked at the age of four years old, then ended up living in a foster home. Later on, Brian battled addictions and other challenges, which we know are a direct "trauma response."

Brian and I became fast friends. One of the kindest and sweetest souls I've ever met. In the beginning of my own recovery, I was hosting an internet radio show on Intention Radio called "The Rx Diaries." Brian kindly agreed to be interviewed for my show. His story was almost unbelievable, yet tales of this type are more common than most people know. It was compelling, chilling, awe inspiring, and probably the most frightening account of abuse and neglect of a child that I had ever heard. As I listened to his account, my stomach tightened, my heart raced, and I felt a rush of tears thinking about what my friend had lived through at the hands of the people who were supposed to protect him. Like many others, I found myself completely engrossed in this sweet soul's account of his "childhood." My heart literally hurt inside of my chest as I listened and tried to process Brian's account of his trauma.

Brian and I both enjoyed our friendship. I went to see him perform locally in The *King and I*. He was a brilliant performer. We took my granddaughter, Rosie, out for lunch in our town. We also spent lots of time texting and talking on the phone, engaging in many, many meaningful, heartfelt conversations, each of us supporting the other in our respective recoveries. Eventually, after Brian moved to Rhode Island (I live in New York), we lost touch, yet I always loved my friend, and my heart smiled whenever he crossed my mind. He was such a great comfort and loving support to me when I had felt completely lost in early 2013, just starting out in my recovery. He was an anchor.

Several years later, I would have the opportunity to be the conduit of Divine support for Brian. God/Spirit/Universe planned a "reunion" for us one late night in 2018, even though we were living states apart—a reunion that would literally save Brian's life.

Restless and unable to sleep, I logged into Facebook to divert my busy mind, and I immediately saw my friend Brian doing a Facebook LIVE. I excitedly clicked on the link, eager to see what my friend was up to, only to witness a horrifying scene. Brian was clearly intoxicated, and he seemed hopeless, helpless, and was experiencing suicidal ideation. He was not making any sense and was escalating in his agitation. He was also clearly delusional. I knew I had a limited window of opportunity to help my dear friend. Brian was spiraling down, LIVE, in real time.

He needed help fast! He lived hours away in Rhode Island. I was unsuccessfully trying to join him on the LIVE and typing in the LIVE comments to get his attention, to guide him, and to let him know I was there, to no avail. Brian was completely oblivious in his mental state and acuity, and was not responding to me. My heart began racing, and all I could do in that moment was to remember my mental health first aid and suicide safety training. I've taught these steps to thousands in my work throughout my community: "Breathe. Remain present in order to be clear in stating the facts, in order to send for help. Speak confidently. **CALL 911.**"

Unfortunately, implementing the **ALGEE** action plan (Mental health First Aid: *Assess for risk of suicide or harm. Listen non-judgmentally. Give reassurance and information. Encourage appropriate professional help. Encourage self-help and other support strategies*), associated with my training and education, where we attempt to administer Mental Health First Aid until help arrives or until the situation is resolved, was not an option. I could not reach my friend via phone, Facebook, or text. I immediately called the police in Brian's town to assist. I calmly explained what I had just observed on Facebook, and that I was a Recovery Specialist who works in the field of mental health, and asked that they go over to Brian's home to do a "wellness check."

Unbeknownst to Brian, he was about to begin a brand-new type of recovery of body, mind, and spirit. I reached out to a friend/colleague who works in the field at a top drug/alcohol/mental health facility in the country who could help him ... *if* Brian made the decision to accept the help.

The very next morning, Brian called me while I was at work at the Mental Health Association. He was deeply grateful for my intervention, which we know was "Divine intervention. We talked for some time, and I suggested that he allow me to guide him in finding the perfect rehabilitation "fit" for him. I explained to Brian that he could begin a "holistic recovery" through an integrated approach aligned with a traditional medical approach. He gratefully agreed.

I stayed close in support of Brian over the next couple of months as he reached out very often to vent, to talk, or to tell me what he was afraid of as he prepared for treatment. I always took his calls, and checked up on him a few times a week while he awaited an empty bed in the facility. Unfortunately, it is like this in every facility across the country, with a break down between "supply and demand." This breakdown could be life threatening, so I gratefully stood in as the "transition" until a bed became available. I knew that, once Brian entered the facility, he would not be allowed to have his phone to continue our communication. I let him know that I would be there in "spirit" and cheering him on in the background, praying for his wellness, and that I would be here when he returned home and was ready to re-connect. I told him that, together, we would one day serve others living with these disorders. Today, both of us have written books to do exactly that, serve others. Brian is doing really well today. Brian has crawled out of the darkness through Spirit's light and grace.

As a young boy being abused, Brian would look up and sing out, "This little light of mine" to connect to Spirit."

Here is what he wrote to me in May, 2021.

"EARTH ANGEL! Oh. Do I have your permission to tell our story, because you threw a buoy...my dear!"

What a blessing to have been chosen by Spirit to help my friend in God's grace! My answer?

"Of course. Anything for you, my dear friend."

Brian went on to thank me for all of the work that I do every day in being of service to those who are living with substance use disorder, and mental illness.

"And bravo for the daily work you DO for guiding our future! Not work for the faint of heart! The work ahead requires complete transparency. Vulnerability. And requires that we lift each other because sometimes we can't lift ourselves!"

God/Spirit/Universe guided and worked through me that night to save Brian's life. This was the purpose that led us to cross paths in 2013, as well as Brian being a gift to me along my own recovery journey. It was also an answer to my daily prayer:

"Today please show me who to see, where to go, what to say, and to whom, to help another person."

As a matter of routine, I am never up at that late hour, and certainly not on Facebook. Spirit is always guiding us and using us to serve and support others. If we are open to Divine communication, we are able to see and hear beyond our physical limitations and truly serve.

Brian is one of my truest inspirations. What an incredible and brave man (and what a journey!). Brian's light is shining once again.

My dear Brian, Spirit heard your voice singing, "This little light of mine" and answered on that late night in 2018.

"Faith that perseveres is faith that is strengthened," and it is food for the soul.

Although I have unhealthy thoughts from time to time, they make sense to me. These thoughts are the product of a memory that is all too familiar, which has been buried deep within my cellular structure from my past: unhealed trauma. When a similar situation occurs, my cellular memory is triggered by a past experience. However, if we can connect to our inner wisdom and our deepest truth, and we are open to peeling back each layer, acknowledging and taking the time to process the trauma, we can assign to it its proper resting place. If we have a Divine "intervention-ist," helping us differentiate between the past and the present, we are able to re-frame our memories, reset our thoughts, and reset our behaviors. Only then are we able to live in the present and allow ourselves to experience new and healthy rational thoughts. These new thought patterns lead us to new, healthy, and rational behaviors, relationships, and choices, which do eventually create a new and healthy lifestyle.

We awaken and transform.

Mindfulness is another imperative tool on my journey of recovery. The energy of mindfulness that we achieve through a meditation practice is a vital source of Spiritual nourishment, and it can significantly speed up and deepen our Spiritual growth. Mindfulness strategies control our internal state through our breath, through movement, and through visualization. We can consciously control our breathing in a mindfulness meditation practice. Respiration and emotional arousal are linked in the brain, so in every moment, your internal state is reflected in your breathing. As a result, our breath is our most effective tool in intervening with our physiology/nervous system in real time! If we calm our breathing, we calm our mind, and vice-versa. We can observe our stress level through our breath in real time, and then use our breath to de-stress in real time!

We have the power!

Chapter 12 will offer more guidance in practicing mindfulness.

And, try the sixty-six-day rule! We know that, if we implement a new healthy practice for sixty-six days, at the same time every day, we will have created a new healthy lifestyle change! The brain does well with predict-ability, repetitive behaviors, and structure!

Replacing unhealthy practices with healthy practices, through awareness and mindfulness, looks like the following, which is the way that I live in my own "wellness approach to recovery." Feel free to use any or all of these practices.

- Worrying and/or Isolating. **Instead**, pray, meditate and have faith. Use any of the prayers within this book that resonate with you to ask for Spirit's grace and guidance. Reach out to a loved one or professional.

- Thinking negative thoughts. **Instead**, practice positive affirmations; say them aloud and to yourself, write them down, and believe in them. Practice non-judgement of yourself. You are doing the best you can with what you have at this moment in time.

- Reacting strictly based on emotions. **Instead**, breathe, observe your feelings/emotions, take a time out to S.P.E.A.R. and follow your S.W.I.M. Recovery plan. (Refer to chapter 6) Find a constructive/mutually beneficial resolution.

- Engaging in relationships that create ongoing stress/anxiety. **Instead**, engage with others who are uplifting, positive, and supportive, and who offer and accept love unconditionally, without drama or judgement. These are relationships that flow with ease.

- Working constantly as a distraction to avoid unpleasant realizations/truths. **Instead**, allow yourself to "feel" your truth, perhaps with a trained professional or trusted loved one. You are allowed to feel whatever you feel! Also enjoy recreation with loved ones. Practice self-care daily.

- Eating in a hurry. **Instead**, practice mindful eating, gratitude for food and for the time to sit in peace, to savor every bite, and to chew and digest food slowly and purposefully.

- Sitting for too long without mindful movement. **Instead**, stand up every thirty minutes, stretch, take a short walk, practice yoga, and tune in to your body's physical needs.

When we practice mindfulness, we bring ourselves into deliberate balance where we thrive in wellness. Wellness is where we stand in our power! Our fundamental awareness and deep intuitive nature speak gently to us when we embrace our truth.

Our integrity is showcased in our decision to meet that truth and to not compromise our love and respect for ourselves or others. It is shown when we continue to hold ourselves to our highest standards in following our Divine path.

This statement confirms my commitment to my wellness. If it resonates with you, feel free to affirm it with me:

Commitment to Recovery Affirmation

I cannot change what happened yesterday, but today is a new day, and I will do my best to remember the lessons of the past. If I falter, please be patient and encourage me. I am a work in progress, learning and growing every day. If I do not do my best today, tomorrow I will try again. Please encourage me kindly and lovingly to continue to seek my highest potential. I will respond lovingly and with gratitude, and I will remember your loving words. Otherwise, all I will remember are the failures of yesterday, which may cause me to continue to fail. Encourage me. Focus on the good and the positive, and that will expand over time.

The best moments are the little, yet profound moments, when we connect with the Universe. Spiritual awareness is where all growth, connection, and healing begin, within ourselves and within our relationships. This is an organic and powerful alliance and a gift through the loving support from, and connection to the Universe. We must dig deeply within to make that connection, to be willing to face ourselves, and to be brave in seeing ourselves authentically. We must be brave in making changes that will allow us to further evolve emotionally and spiritually. This is where the work begins, and it is a lifelong educational commitment. We must remain open to becoming Spiritual students. Every day, we open the channels of communication that guide us to live a life in which we discover the energy of our own unique spirit and our own power. We can achieve an awareness of our highest self through conversations in meditation and prayer with the Universe/God/Spirit. These are a deep and meaningful source of little, yet monumental moments. These moments have the power to elevate our awareness to a higher level, which creates a transformation of the human spirit.

I remind myself each day of my wellness recovery, that I am doing my absolute best, that we all need validation now and again, and that it is all in God's plan. I trust that whatever and whomever are meant to help me will show up at the perfect time. In the meantime, I continue to be an astute, eager, and loving spiritual student practicing daily self-care.

Spirit's Advice on Supporting Recovery

Spirit has guided me to pass on this advice: "When helping one who is lost and attempting to find their way, offer empathy and non-judgmental listening and support as they continue on their journey of self-discovery. Hold the space for them to experience a profound spiritual connection, and for them to dig deeply until they courageously pry open all that darkens their inner peace that which obscures their opportunity to experience self-love and complete self-honesty. Only a true connection to self, and to Spirit, will provide freedom to self-awareness, which connects us to all the rest. We hold the light for them so that when they explore their own darkness, they will see that they are not alone.

Uncertainty tends to encourage us to stay where we feel safe. When we take a leap of faith guided by the Universe's loving guidance, we are certain of Divine blessings and begin to truly experience spiritual awareness through the lens of love led by faith, hope, and trust.

What we see from our point of view influences our reality. Widen the lens. Once we open ourselves to self-exploration, as well as other people's perspectives, we are able to open our minds to many possibilities. We have a choice as to how we see, how we think, how we react, how we interact, and how we choose to live our lives. As we learn, we grow and expand our consciousness, becoming empowered to reach a higher level of awareness. *A Course In Miracles* says, "Open-mindedness comes with lack of judgement."

As an evolving woman, I am always open to change, and I have the opportunity to change the trajectory of my own journey. Throughout our journey, we sharpen our awareness as we become more connected to our intuition and live aligned with our truth, unapologetically led by the Universe/God/Spirit. Our recovery and our new healthy lifestyle begins to flow organically and naturally once we experience our connection to our true self (our spiritual awakening) and we employ an open mindset, in which change and growth move us to evolve. We become eager to do the work. Our blessings multiply. And we pay it forward.

Write about three things that came to you this week that you were unable to awaken to until you began your spiritual practice of connecting to self. How have they changed your path?
Your relationship to self? Your life? Your insight? Your relationships? Your overall health? Your mental health?

_____

_____

_____

_____

_____

What do you remember feeling physically in your body the last time you began to experience anxiety, depression, anger, sadness? How did you navigate those feelings? What might you do differently the next time you begin to move on the continuum towards feeling unwell? Remember, we all have mental health!

Prepare your plan in advance! Use the S.W.I.M. method in Chapter 6. Our best self-care is awareness and prevention.

_____

_____

_____

_____

_____

_____

How has your practice of self-love, self-care, self-assessment, self-awareness, self-regulation, and self-respect improved on your spiritual path?

_____

_____

_____

_____

_____

Since you have begun to live aligned with your own truth, what has changed?

_____

_____

_____

_____

_____

What are you most proud of this week? What would you like to work on based on your experiences this week to achieve a more spiritually aligned outcome?

_____

_____

_____

_____

Going forward, how could you do even more to support the positive changes in your life?

_____

_____

_____

_____

_____

_____

What is your "go-to" self-care practice(s) as you "check in" with yourself daily? What other practices are you willing to try?

_____

_____

_____

_____

_____

_____

CHAPTER 11

Vision: I See, Hear, And Feel Beyond My Physical Limitations

"The Knowing...Always and Forever"

Recently, a very wise healer/intuitive told me not to doubt my intuition. I knew exactly what he meant. I have known for most of my life that I am blessed with a gift of Spiritual "knowing" and intuition. It is Divine direction and guidance, as the Universe interacts with me through many paths of higher communication. In the years of recovery from my prescription drug addiction, and co-occurring mental health disorders, my Spiritual connection has become stronger than ever. My senses are in a heightened state of awareness and receiving. I am blessed to be fully awake to experience all of the beautiful and meaningful moments of life, as well as those I am made aware of beyond my physical limitations.

A recent Spiritual encounter happened in January of 2020, where I was shown very specific information. I had been missing Steve, my ex, who had been my love for a very long time. At this time, although we kept in touch intermittently, we had been apart for two years after being together for three years, on and off. Steve and I had been madly in love and committed to each other, but we both brought unhealed trauma into our current relationship, which made it painful and difficult to navigate. Often, we would inadvertently be triggered by each other, and each time, it became more difficult to recover. We sought short-term therapy, to no avail. We separated on January 13, 2018. We were both seriously heart-broken. Neither of us had the tools at that time to navigate our differences selflessly, simultaneously practicing self-care while caring for our beloved. Neither of us had healed enough yet from previous stress and trauma, and each time we differed, it drained us both of our energy. Recovering from these conflicts was even more challenging with each event. All along, Spirit had been reassuring me that Steve and I would find our way back to each other.

Steve would intermittently keep in touch, and we would profess our love for each other. I would send him love energetically multiple times a day, and I could feel him intuitively receiving my love. However, we must always live by Divine timing. I could feel the deep, loving, Spiritual energy between us every day. I never doubted that, at the perfect time, the Universe would orchestrate this reunion. Steve and I would find each other again, and led by Spirit, we would know at that time if we were meant to be together for a season, or a lifetime. I knew we would forever be connected energetically, steeped in love, guided by the Divinity within us, and always blessed by Spirit to have shared love, time, and space, even if it were to be temporary. In January 2020, the synchronicities and messages from Spirit communicated clearly that Steve and I would be brought together on January 17, 2020. These signs were exactly what I had envisioned and believed with certainty.

It bears repeating: *A Course In Miracles* reminds us that "Those who are certain of the outcome can afford to wait and wait without anxiety." This has become my mantra over the years, which is why I repeat it so often in this book. Although I missed Steve terribly, I was certain of the outcome of seeing him at least once more. I was also prepared to let him go, if Spirit communicated that this would be in our highest blessings. I would trust the process. I would trust that God/Spirit/Universe knows what would serve us at this time in our lives. I would wait for that information. I lived my life every moment to the fullest, in joy, in the present moment, with family, friends, and work, waiting with a full expectation of a miracle for us to meet again, whether for a short time, or for our "always and forever."

Steve had come into my life in December of 2014, not quite two years into my recovery. He was there to guide me and to cheer me on during so many life lessons. I valued his insight and life wisdom. He used to call me a "butterfly." I broke out of the darkness of my chrysalis, and wings in tow, was free … as a butterfly. When we would awaken in the morning, he would smile that beautiful smile with his gorgeous dimple and say, "Good morning, sunshine!" And, as he kissed me goodbye at the door as I left for work, he would always say, "Go save lives." He was so proud of me and the work that I was doing. When I returned home, he'd say, "How was your day? And don't leave out any details!" Steve was my best friend and the love of my life. He could make me laugh like no other. We had a special prayer that we prayed every morning, and even when we were in different physical locations, we would pray together over the phone. I had never loved so deeply before, or connected so deeply and spiritually with anyone, and certainly not since. I am at peace, knowing that I had a true love experience, and I enjoy my life, solo, for now, with my family and friends, and my career, serving as many as God entrusts to me in my community.

On January 17, 2020, as the day went on, the signs from the Universe/God/Spirit, became more and more apparent, through music, through other people's words, and through my intuition. I had been invited by my friends Jason and Annie to attend a music event. I "knew" that Steve would be there. I could feel it in my gut. Our song, "At Last," had been playing throughout the last week, more than usual, followed by a stream of "reunion" music offering confirmation, and a week prior, a car had passed me on my way home from work with the license plate "Atlast2."

Steve's name, first and last, also continued to reveal itself to me, and our number "555" as well. Steve is of Latin descent (we used to lovingly call each other "Lucy and Ricky,") and on my Pandora radio, between songs, commercials were aired in Spanish, Steve's heritage. For a few days, it was constant influx of messages. Daily signs, messages, and synchronicity from Spirit showed up. I was beyond excited as I longed to see Steve once more, no matter the outcome.

As I pulled into the venue to meet Jason and Ann, I once again heard our song play on Pandora. I also asked the Universe, on my drive there, to show me our number, 555, if in fact my intuition was correct (Steve's birth month and birth year) for further validation. As I pulled up to the light before the venue, a truck pulled alongside of me with a license plate with the last three numbers 555! Then as I said thank you to Spirit and started to get very emotional, loud sirens began to blow from the firehouse right where I was driving. In the past, Spirit has made loud declarations in this way! (Spirit is not always subtle!) I was getting so excited! I could not wait to see Steve. I was experiencing that "certainty and knowing!" It was thrilling! We hadn't seen each other in so long! As I was about to get out of my car, I could see a car begin to back up into the space next to me. It was dark, but I could see the license plate and make of the car, and my heart began to race with excitement. There was Steve behind the wheel! He saw me, looked shocked, and motioned for me to approach. I actually felt lightheaded and began to feel faint as I approached my beloved. In fact, I think I lost my balance for a moment! I was nervous and excited at the same time. Everything that I "knew" to be true and that I was certain of through Spiritual communication had come to fruition. I had dreamed about and prayed for this day.

That night was a reminder and validation that everything that I feel and believe, energetically and spiritually, is a manifestation of my positivity, my beliefs, and my gorgeous spiritual practice that keeps me connected to the truth through the loving guidance of the Universe/God/Spirit. Steve and I danced, we flirted, we laughed, and we hugged. With us, and our deep soul love, we don't need words to feel the love. We are love, and in love with each other, and it is palpable to us and to anyone in our company. All night long, we "danced," our dance. Heart to heart. Soul to soul. Pure love.

A few months later, Spirit revealed to me that Steve and I were only fated for a season. I trust that there is a Divine blessing in this separation. I may never know what that is, but my faith is so strong that I "know" it is for both Steve's and my highest good. We have been so blessed to have found each other and to share the time and experiences that we had enjoyed as a couple, and with our beautiful children and grandchildren.

Even when people leave our lives physically, love always keeps them close in memory, and in matters of the heart, and soul.

Update: Yet again, Steve and I re-connected in September of 2021. Steve visited me after sixteen long months of no contact. It was a beautiful blessing of closure, or what it seemed was closure... But then, less than two weeks later, Steve reached out again. We spent a meaningful and beautifully blessed day together filled with love, closeness, and memories. I had been given the exact date of Thursday, Sept. 23, 2021 by my psychic that Steve was going to contact me. It came to fruition. And, I was told that he was going to speak his truth to me, and he did. Once again, Spirit had been sending me definite signs in the most recent past that validated my psychic's intuition. Moreover, my own intuition is so strong, so deeply connected to the Universe, that it was of no surprise to me when Steve reached out to me. On the morning of September 23rd, as I went on my daily walk around the pond, thinking about Steve and praying for him and his family, "looking up" to Spirit, I asked for information about Steve that I should know. A song that I had never heard before began playing on Pandora called, "Your Mother," (I knew this was my dear mother, my angel in Heaven speaking to me) by Menken from Beauty and the Beast, followed by Jim Brickman's "New Beginnings," then "Touched By An Angel," by Ametria, then "My Saving Grace," by Mariah Carey, then "Praise Him," by Lenny LeBlanc, and finally, ending with "Timing Is Everything" by Chris DeBurgh.

I had a "knowing." I knew that my late mother was communicating with me. I could "feel" Steve's presence through my mother's spiritual presence and guidance.

Five minutes after the last song, Steve's email came through on my iPhone as I continued my walk around the pond.

"Thy Will Be Done."

Amen.

Steve visited, and we both shared our deep feelings of love for each other.

I always said that whatever God felt was best for both of us, "Thy Will Be Done." And I am at peace with whatever that is. He, after all, knows what is best. I trust Him implicitly.

Thoughts On Envisioning, "Knowing," And Spiritual Signs

We co-create our masterpieces. Envision it daily, stand firm in a spiritual practice that resonates with you, believe with certainty all that you *"know"*, and wait patiently in excitement and certainty. Communication with Spirit is my most treasured time of each and every day, even if the message doesn't align with my desires. I am certain that Spirit is demonstrating unconditional love the likes of which I have never before experienced. I have unwavering faith that Spirit is bringing forth my highest blessings. This is the grounding principle of the foundation of my wellness.

My writing is also an important principle of my wellness. It has given me a voice. It is a reflection of the deepest part of my soul. It expresses the inner beauty and monumental growth within, spiritual lessons, life lessons, stillness and peace, and the divinity within that has offered healing from the cracks that once fractured my foundation. Those cracks are now barely visible to others, yet are always a reminder of my ongoing journey. I am well. I am safe. I am always in the company of the Divine.

I am not always certain of my path, yet I know where I am headed, one slow and purposeful step at a time.

Our perspective is what we choose to see. Observe beyond your physical limitations. This is the space where we receive Divine opportunities, and are extended the honor to co-create.

CHAPTER 12
Faith and Spirituality ... My Way

"Awakening moment"

I*n the recent past, I chose to rebuild my life and create the life that I envision for me—not what others said "should be."* Mama Sheila (Sheila Pearl), my loving "soul mama," mentor, coach, spiritual advisor, and confidante, always says, "Don't *should* all over yourself!" I tore down the existing structure (my fear-based comfort zone). With purpose, determination, vision, confidence, and faith, I faced all of my fears and single-handedly, one brick at a time, began to rebuild. I felt fearful, but I did it anyway. I took risks. I am living the life I envisioned for myself. Fear is a choice created by thoughts, and thoughts are not facts—they are fleeting feelings in response to conditioning.

In the beginning of my recovery, I sought out advice—from everyone, including family, friends, and even mere acquaintances—on every decision I was about to make. At times, I allowed my fear to overtake my faith in myself, and in God. At the beginning of my early recovery, I often felt I was on shaky ground and did not trust my intuition. Unsurprisingly, I found that every single person I asked for advice or opinions differed from each other and from me. After a short while, I realized that the Universe/God/Spirit orchestrated this confusion in order to remind of my deep

Spiritual connection, which was my catalyst in seeking help for recovery, and that it was all I needed as I sought guidance.

As fearful as I felt in speaking my truth about my addiction, on April 3, 2013, I was even more fearful of losing my battle and leaving behind my precious children and my only granddaughter at that time, Rosie. I asked for God's grace, strength, and guidance, and by the grace of God, took the initial step in asking for help to save my life. When I finally spoke up, I felt empowered. I felt an even deeper Spiritual connection.

My best friends of over forty years, Bill and Vicky Kelder, were right there with me for the entire journey. They observed me in a complete mental breakdown, where I was incoherent and telling them all about the things I believed to be true (including that my husband was trying to kill me) just weeks before I asked for help. When I went to the hospital to detox, they took care of everything that needed to get done so that I would not have any responsibilities to distract me during my initial stage of recovery. Vicky visited me to bring me some clothes, but was not allowed through the double steel doors that separated us. We waved to each other through the little window. I felt like a prisoner, and in a way, I was.

When I returned home from rehab, I sought out advice (an old pattern of unhealthy behavior) from so many! I asked everything from "Where should I live now?" to "What should I do to earn a living?" to "What type of recovery practice do you think I should implement into my life?" The people at the recovery centers (yes, there were two of them) where I did my rehab said that I "had to attend twelve-step meetings in order to recover properly." I remember my life coach at that time, Maria Blon, a beautiful and kind soul, said to me, "Only do what feels right for you," when I expressed to her that I did not want to go these meetings as they did not resonate with me. I had wanted to explore and experience a holistic lifestyle using natural and organic solutions. Maria's words gave me the strength and encouragement that I needed to begin my exploration and discovery of what I soon learned was an untapped pathway to recovery. Here is where my "Wellness Approach to Recovery" program was born.

During this time of seeking out so many opinions from others, I felt like I was on an endless hamster wheel. Fortunately, with Maria's ongoing guidance, I decided to turn back to my faith through writing, praying, and meditation. We all falter at times. However, when we catch ourselves, and we are resilient through constant healthy practices and repetitive actions that reinforce our strength and our faith, it becomes a lifestyle. A therapist suggested that I was "depressed," and that medication would be helpful for me. I disagreed, as my body was finding its "new normal." I had no intention of taking pills to regulate my brain ever again. Look where doing so had gotten me!

I knew inherently what I needed to heal, and what I did not need.

I was up every day, eating, going to work, working through my feelings with my life coach, Maria, feeling healthy, and yes, finding my way.

About a year and a half into my recovery, I had met and fallen in love with Steve. My therapist at that time discouraged me from the relationship, saying that she did not think I was "ready." I left her practice, because at that time, I didn't feel she was serving me in my best interest. However, years later, I did return for a brief period of time when Steve and I were experiencing challenges, and my mother became gravely ill and passed away. I still work with my therapist as unhealed trauma rears its ugly head now and then, and I ask for support and assignments to help me "heal deeper." I have learned that, even in therapy, we can take what resonates for us, and just say no to what does not. We do not need to walk away completely, as long as we use our voice to stand in our own power to speak our truth, and to express what we know we need. Inherently, we all know what we need.

Initially leaving this therapist's practice because I did not like her input relates back to what I had learned as a child. If you don't like something, just leave. Give up. Leave them if they dare to disagree. Don't give it a second thought.

I have learned to "take what works and leave the rest." In *every* situation, there will be something that doesn't resonate with us. We can't walk away from every situation. We need to be open and flexible. Healing from trauma is a lifelong process, and I am all in. I want to heal, to grow, to evolve, and to be a shining example of what recovery and wellness truly looks like, feels like, and is: awareness, self-regulation, balance, and self-care steeped in spiritual solutions. This IS recovery. I have a great support system, and my greatest support and direction comes from the Universe/God/Spirit. As I remain alert and awake and willing to embrace my spirituality, ongoing, I understand more and more deeply why my life was saved on April 3, 2013.

With Spirit as my guide, I never feel the temptation or need, in any circumstance, to self-medicate. Spirit is my strength. Spirit always has my back. Spirit is my alignment. Spirit is within, and Spirit is all around. Listen, look, and feel beyond your physical limitations. Experience this miracle: With just a simple shift in perception, we are always in the presence of a higher source of energy. It is never "me." It is always "we." A loving, guiding, powerful, and knowing higher source that teaches us and provides us with our highest blessings, if we are open to this gorgeous presence.

The healing you seek begins in your soul. Inherently, each of us knows what we need to heal, and daily spiritual self-care practices help me to tap into that "knowing." They keep me grounded, connected, and in a beautiful and deep alignment with myself and with Spirit. If any of the following resonates with you, feel free to adapt to your daily practice:

1. Daily early morning meditation/prayer, where I seek loving guidance.

2. One-minute "realignment" meditations as needed throughout the day.

3. Fifteen to thirty minutes of free writing in my journal, including gratitude for spiritual connection, based on my early morning meditation/prayer experience, and writing a daily inspirational blog on www.writeprayrecover.com.

4. Taking a walk with the intention of mindfully observing the beauty that surrounds me, while mindfully breathing, and taking photographs of what inspires me.

5. Staying connected to others in a way that is cathartic for my soul, as well as offering healing and support to others.

6. Listening and connecting to music or an inspiring audiobook.

7. Eating mindfully and choosing foods that promote wellness, including plenty of water.

8. Practicing empathy and compassion, utilizing a judgement-free mindset of myself and others.

9. Using essential oils in a diffuser, or inhaling the oils in a deep breathing exercise.

10. Cooking and baking, and creating new gluten free recipes.

11. Unplugging from social media in long "chunks" throughout the day and replacing screen time with face-to-face or phone connection, or just silence. *I absolutely LOVE silence! And silence is where I hear the loudest spiritual direction.*

I always end my day in prayer and/or mindfulness practices. These include a **gratitude prayer** and a **body-scan meditation/mindful breathing strategy** which are effective for stress reduction, relaxation, wellness, and physical, emotional, and spiritual awareness.

I use a "gratitude prayer" that is as simple as I can make it, and yet it is powerful in reminding myself of my blessings, says, "Thank you," to God/Spirit/Universe for bestowing blessings on me, and realigns me with His will:

> *"Thank you for your loving presence, guidance, support,*
> *and protection today, for all of my blessings, and most of all,*
> *for my loving connection to You."*

A body scan is a simple yet powerful type of mindfulness strategy that allows one to observe, or to "scan" their body, one body part at a time, in order to be cognizant of how one is feeling. If one chooses to do more than "scan," they may breathe into any tightness or uncomfortable feelings, which will soften that area of the body and promote relaxation and an overall feeling of wellness. You may want to accompany the "scan" with a relaxation/mindfulness app like "Calm" (or one of your own choice), as well as relaxing music, or even listening to a *"Gong Bath"* music accompaniment. A *"Gong Bath"* offers a "psycho-acoustic gateway to heightened states of awareness and consciousness. The frequencies surpass the intellectual part of the brain and travel to the core of the cellular system where the healing qualities are fully absorbed." I find it extremely healing. You can Google "Gong Bath" and find many on YouTube, or you can find one in my free S.P.E.A.R. and S.W.I.M. into Wellness E-Book on my website www.harmonioushealth4life.com.

Body-Scan Meditation:

Observe how you are feeling physically as you "SCAN" each body part.

One at a time, bring your attention to the top of your head, your face, shoulders, arms, hands, chest, tummy, legs, feet. Just observe how each body part feels as you scan. Tight or relaxed? Clenched or soft?

Next, purposefully relax your forehead, open your jaw and let it fall, relax your facial muscles, and relax your shoulders, if they are pulled up to your ears (we do this when we feel stressed, and when we do, it also tightens our neck, which may cause neck and back pain), drop them from your ears to sit in a relaxed state.

How does your chest feel? You can put one hand on your chest, and one on your tummy to scan.

Let your belly relax and continue to scan the rest of your body all the way down to your feet, one body part at a time. Just notice. Are your hands clenched into fists, or resting softly in your lap? Are your feet "floppy" in your shoes, or do they feel curled up and tight? How do your legs feel?

Now, that you have scanned, choose a "breathing cavity" of your choice where you can focus as your breath goes in and out. (Mouth, tummy, chest, nose) and begin a *"box breathing"* for about three minutes, focusing on your breath, and visualizing the in-and-out, or up-and-down movement of that cavity. Lastly, at the same time, in alignment with your breathing, insert a positive thought or a positive visual into your space that makes you smile or feel peaceful. It can be a simple thought, such as "I know that I am safe." Or "My loved ones are my joy." In addition, or alternately, you may choose to visualize a place, person, or situation that brings you joy. Focus on this visual throughout your box breathing.

Positive affirmations and imagery, and mindful breathing, combined with a relaxation/mindfulness strategy, set in a quiet space where we feel safe, resets the brain from fearful, stressful, and worrisome thoughts to calming, uplifting, and happy thoughts!

Reset and realign with these spiritual solutions and self-care practices that are so easily accessible.

Deepening And Trusting in Spiritual Guidance

This statement confirms my commitment to my spirituality. If it resonates with you, feel free to affirm it with me:

> "I will not concern myself with how many twists and turns the road takes on the way to my desired destination. It IS all about the journey. This is my opportunity to practice commitment to my faith and to all that I believe to be true. I will continue to stay deeply connected to the Universe/God/Spirit while navigating the uncertainty."

No matter how many situations have presented themselves that appeared dismal and dark, I have stood deeply in my faith, and I have witnessed sudden miracles of resolution that have become my blessings.

Proceed with confidence, purpose, and courage. Embrace the twists and turns, for they are where character is built, and where faith becomes the foundation of our lives.

Your path is not a one-way street. Where there is an entrance, there is an exit, or even an opportunity to turn around and begin again. Listen and see beyond your physical limitations for Divine directions.

As you connect daily to the deepest part of yourself and to the Universe, you will begin to notice a shift. You will begin to feel empowered, for when we are aligned to truth and faith, Spirit is always present.

Each day as you begin a spiritual practice that resonates with you, choose one challenging event or situation that you are experiencing, and write down one step you have taken, or are willing to take, to align with Spirit through acknowledgment of your truth. As you connect daily to the deepest part of yourself through your truth, and to the Universe in alignment with deep faith and trust, you will begin to notice a shift. You'll begin to feel empowered. When we are aligned, Spirit is always present.

"As you take each spiritually aligned step, write down what you notice. Do you feel joy and love? Do you feel hopeful? Are you experiencing anxiety? Even in the challenges and adversity, are you "certain" of the outcome, which will be for your highest good? This all takes time and practice, so go slowly. As my son, Matthew states, "Slow and steady wins the race."

Do you stand firmly in your faith even though there may be a distracting cacophony of "white noise" going on in the background? Do you have faith in your "knowing?" Write about any experience where distractions presented themselves, and yet you stood in your faith.

_____

_____

_____

_____

_____

When you begin to feel fear, are you resilient, in that you ask God/Universe/Spirit to redirect you back to alignment on His path? To reinterpret for you what you "think" you are experiencing to the actual truth of the experience? Simply asking for this redirection, and getting still to listen for Spirit's answer is aligning in and of itself. Can you readily get back on track with ease and confidence through this practice? Write about it!

_____

_____

_____

_____

_____

Each day, first thing in the morning, allow yourself to be Divinely guided in prayer and/or meditation for the day ahead. This guidance creates a shift to awareness, truth and peace. Once you receive your guidance, write it down as a blueprint for the day. Give specific examples of how you may implement Spirit's suggested guidance. (Writing, a walk in nature, volunteering to serve others, etc.) Memorialize them, and use them as an "at a glance" reference point for any future spiritual solution suggestions that you may need.

_____

_____

_____

_____

_____

_____

_____

_____

_____

_____

_____

_____

_____

Some days you may continue to remain in the step from the day before. That's okay! Whenever you are ready to take the next step, meditate to go within and ask the Universe to reveal your next move. Listen to your intuition. Always take your time with this. It is not a competition. Whatever is comfortable for you on your own journey is the "right pace in the right space." Be consistent in your practice. When you ask for loving guidance, the Universe will always provide answers. On the days in which you remained in a "paused" state, or a "resting" state, how did you stay spiritually connected and aligned? Write it all down!

_____

_____

_____

_____

_____

_____

_____

_____

_____

_____

_____

_____

CHAPTER 13

Surrender

"The Peace of Knowing"

O ver the years of my life, desperately wanting a specific outcome in my marriage, in my career, relationships, and many other life circumstances, I exhausted myself physically, mentally, and spiritually in trying to force every outcome. I would try to manipulate the outcome that I felt I "knew" was best for me or that I wanted, to no avail. Clearly, an illusion. I had not yet learned my greatest lesson: Surrender.

As my own life hung in the balance on that day of awakening in 2013, I was certain that I was being supported and held in God's loving embrace. When the ambulance took me to the hospital on the day, I was in grave health. I was in and out of consciousness and in severe withdrawal from codeine pills, Xanax, and many other controlled substances. I was severely dehydrated, as well as malnourished, due to a severe eating disorder. But, when I came to, I remember feeling a sense of peace. I remember speaking aloud to Spirit and saying, "I surrender. I am not afraid." I knew that whatever was meant to be—whether I might live or die—it would be for the highest good. I did not beg for my life. I just "knew" that I had not been brought this far on my life path to be taken now, because I had heard God say so when I prayed to him the night before, asking Him to show me the way out. After the constant struggle, frustration, mental and physical illness caused by this pointless tug-of-war, and then reminding myself of a quote that was so apropos, "Your arm's too short to box with God!" (Amen), I surrendered.

Surrender is the ultimate freedom because it is a rejection of the illusion that we have control over our lives. Only the Universe/Spirit/God has that kind of control, and it is exhausting to try to take that onto your own human shoulders. My addiction was one element of that false control, and I nearly paid the price with my life. All mechanisms of false control are only destined to fail and to exhaust you in the process. What a relief it was to give up this illusion!

Through daily radical acceptance of whatever circumstances present themselves, and daily alignment with Spirit throughout the years of my recovery, I would become my healthiest self. The Universe has never disappointed me with its gorgeous blessings. In fact, many were blessings I could never have imagined for myself.

Most recently, I was struggling financially and considered returning to teaching, which is one of my passions. I had hoped it could allow me to earn a better living. I prayed for guidance, and through a conversation with my friend Karen, Spirit suggested I apply for a teaching position. I went into the interview very prepared, but I had absolutely *no* expectations. After all, I was sixty-one-years-old, and I thought they would go for someone younger with more recent experience. However, the Universe is always in control of our destiny and has a plan! I began seeing the name of the city where I was eventually to be hired everywhere! I knew that the Universe was reassuring me that not only would I soon have this new job, but I would also be able to crawl out of debt while doing the work I was passionate about within my community. I wanted to work with youth in circumstances similar to mine growing up. As a person who had overcome the same struggles, who would be better than me to guide them?! Not only did I get this new job, but I was also asked to work with our teacher's center at extra pay. Because of this, teachers who attended my workshops would receive professional credits! Can you say blessing, blessing, blessing?!

Amen! Amen! Amen!

I simply listened to the Spiritual guidance that I was receiving, opened my mindset to new perspectives (the miracle shift), and was guided through Spiritual solutions to choices that would not only enhance my career, but would also allow me to serve, which is my passion and my mission!

The moment I surrendered, prayed, believed, and trusted in the loving presence of the Universe/God/Spirit, I received abundance! I do believe that the years of my own "wellness recovery," my extensive training in mental health and substance use disorder and social emotional learning, and all of my successes, challenges, detours, and "un-successes," led me to this new challenge of working with inner city youth. I consider myself so deeply blessed, and I am so grateful. I was thrilled to create new professional development techniques in response to COVID19 and the discussion of mental health issues, trauma, and racial inequity that it has stimulated. Talk about Divine timing! My knowledge and training were being requested, by Spirit, to be shared with my community at this devastating time. It is a win/win for everyone.

Learning to adapt to and appreciate what is, "knowing it is in our highest blessing," is acceptance. Radical acceptance. Attempting to force any circumstances actually diminishes one's self-respect and compromises one's self-love. It also blocks our faith. When a situation is supposed to come to fruition (and in time it eventually does), then we know that the Universe has strategized and planned to place us on our path wherever we were meant to be all along. Even though we cannot "see" the proof that Spirit is working in the best interests of all, it is the peace of surrender that sustains our faith in hard times.

I am now a much sought after mental health and wellness coach, consultant, and educator. In addition to all of this, I also sit on a coalition that serves to educate, empower, and save the lives of our youth. We teach them about substance use disorder and mental illness as we raise awareness in the public through our understanding of the facts of these brain disorders. Once I learned to surrender, all of my highest blessings and those I might offer to others blossomed organically—the way that all beautiful and healthy things emerge.

Suggestions in Practicing Surrender

Even after a hard fall, you accept that there is no other way to travel but to get back on the bike and pedal forward. You pick yourself up, get back on the bike, and resume your journey with caution. With eyes wide open, you hold on. You are ready for the new adventure, and ready to explore all of the beauty and possibilities that the Universe will place in your path. This is your ride. You can choose the speed you're comfortable with as you listen to your inner GPS (**G**od's **P**lan of **S**urrender), and you navigate the terrain with ease, wonder, and purpose. If you want to, you can peel out, burn rubber, make sparks fly, or just coast, but most importantly, you can enjoy the ride!

It is a deep and connected feeling we experience that tells us that the Universe's plan for us, and all that we desire (a co-creation) is unfolding. We experience feelings of a Source, or force, pulling us like a magnet to metal, and we cannot break free of the current. With time, we begin to feel euphoric and grateful in the knowledge that the highest good is coming to fruition. When aligned with the love and guidance of the Universe, we will be amazed at our own power to create opportunities to help ourselves and the world around us.

Ironically, when we believe that all we have is crumbling into pieces, that we have been left with *nothing*, we may finally be able to *surrender*, and in that space of clarity we see *everything* that we need.

When we surrender to God/Universe/Spirit, we are trusting that we are being Divinely guided on a path that will serve our highest blessings. It is not possible for a human being to see or know all that the Universe can, so we must place our trust in the direction we receive. When we stand in that faith and connection, Spirit uses that channel to vibrate meaning through a variety of modalities (Signs? Feelings in your body? A voice? Visions? A "knowing"?) specific to your relationship. Tune in. You will learn quite quickly the "lines of communication" that are open between you. The more you communicate, the more Spirit will respond to you. Now you have an ongoing dialogue! This will assist you in remaining in the present moment, deepening your faith, and in guiding you to remain awake and aware of your connection.

What modalities does Spirit use to communicate with you personally? How do you communicate with Spirit? (Signs? Feelings in your body? A voice? Visions? A "knowing"?) Take notes about this, so you can review and mark any changes that occur over time.

_____

_____

_____

_____

_____

_____

_____

_____

_____

_____

_____

When you are stepping away from faith and begin to feel fear escalating, ask the Universe, "What action would best serve me in this moment?" Then get still and listen to your intuition as you connect to your loving and enlightened guides, and your own "knowing." Did you sense a reply? Write it below.

_____

_____

_____

_____

_____

_____

_____

Ask for a specific sign that will be especially meaningful to you. Write down the sign you have asked for. Wait patiently for it. Allow your intuition to be your guide. When you receive it, memorialize it below, or in your own journal.

_____

_____

_____

_____

_____

_____

_____

Since beginning your spiritual practice, in what ways have you surrendered? How has it freed you? Served you? What have you learned through the practice of surrender? How has it shaped your thinking or behavior?

_____

_____

_____

_____

_____

_____

_____

_____

Since you have surrendered, have you noticed any improved physical health changes along the way? (Less headaches? Less gastrointestinal symptoms? Feeling freer and lighter within? More energy?)

_____

_____

_____

_____

_____

_____

_____

CHAPTER 14

Love As My Inspiration - A Dedication Page

"Inspiration"

I am awakened by a song that deeply and profoundly touches my heart, and I cry. The song is called, "In My Daughter's Eyes" sung by Martina McBride.

In my recovery from SUD, I continue to be inspired by the love of my children, as well as my beautiful granddaughter, Rosie, who turned thirteen on June 3, 2021, and my beautiful new granddaughter, Harper, born May 19, 2021. Their support inspires me to become who I have always wanted to be as a mom, and as a grandmother. It has also led me to become the woman that I am today, and of whom I am very proud. It is a journey that begs for direction and hope through sharing my own story of recovery, and has led to understanding and respecting boundaries as a part of self-care, self-respect, and self-love. As we have rebuilt our relationships, time has been our greatest gift. Sometimes, we may not see eye to eye, and may even keep our distance as part of our self-care, but it is only an illusion, as love, deep family love, knows no space or time. Love transcends separation. We are always connected.

I am grateful for the opportunity to create a life for my adult children, my granddaughters, and myself that offers us deep love, connection, and purpose on our new path, which we continue to carve out as we travel on

our independent and collective journeys. For me, what is most important is to create a legacy that will offer my children and granddaughters a
strong sense of faith, hope, and pride in their heritage, in a God/Spirit/
Universe of their own understanding and choice, and in what I create in
their honor, which speaks of gratitude for a second chance, and of the
deep love—the power of love—between a mother and her precious children, and grandchildren.

To my precious daughter, Nicole:

I look at you and see myself.

I see my soulmate, my kindred Spirit, and beauty that is so deep within,
emerging from your soul.

I see the strength of a hero who carries on every day, even in the toughest
battles, and still smiles.

I see a little girl who was forced to grow up too quickly and encountered
so much despair, yet no matter how much it hurts, she continues to
choose life.

I see a young woman, my beautiful daughter, my best friend, whose soul
reflects back at me. It is so easy to see because our bond is cemented,
our souls connected, and our hearts affected by unconditional love. We
are one.

I see a soul full of love, compassion, kindness, and creativity with the
inner strength to heal herself and others.

I see a survivor who is not sailing away from the storm but learning to
navigate her ship as best she can, finding her way, even as the waves rock
her, sometimes knocking her overboard. She is resourceful, she swims,
she floats back to shore, and regains her balance, setting sail once again.

I see so many small steps in the right direction leading to the bigger
staircase. Take your time, tiptoe gingerly, breathe, have faith in God and
yourself, and take each new step in stride.

I see a butterfly ready to break out of the confines of her chrysalis, embracing her freedom and ready to fly into unexpected glory.

I love you to the moon and back, my beautiful Colie. Always and forever.

To my beautiful daughter, Olivia Rae:

I look at you and am in awe of your beauty, inside and out. With the adversity and challenges that were forced upon you in your life, you have risen above it all gracefully, with strength, with pride, with so much determination, and with your beautiful smile, which is my light. You stayed the course and have co-created a magnificent life for yourself, which now includes your beautiful little family: your loving husband, Matt, and your newborn baby girl, Harper Sydney. I follow you from a distance, yet remain very close as you continue on your path to be sure that you are well cared for and happy, and I see that you are thriving. Each time you reach out to ask for my advice, my heart overflows with love and gratitude. You are my daughter, my friend, and will always be my baby. We have come a long way. My light becomes brighter. *You* are the reason I continue on my journey even during the challenging times. You inspire me. You have given me strength and determination. My love for you is infinite, and our bond is forever cemented in love. You are always in my heart no matter how far apart we are, as we are always connected energetically. There is no space or time when it comes to love, especially between mother and child. I love you too much, my Livee Rae. "I'll love you forever. I'll like you for always. As long as I'm living, my baby you'll be."

For my son-in-law, Matt:

You have been a supportive and loving "son" throughout the years of my recovery. We are family. Thank you for always remaining connected to me in such a loving and devoted way. Love you, sweetie.

For Deb and Art Friedson:

Thank you both for your loving support throughout my years of recovery. Deb, we always say that we are soul sisters, and kindred spirits, and we most certainly are. We are so spiritually aligned. We are family. YOU are my sister. We are Harper's grandmothers, and we always have each other's highest blessings at heart for our beautiful family. We were brought together for the highest blessings of both of our families, and each other. We are now one. I love you so much.

For my loving soul daughter, Sarah:

You were brought into my life as an unexpected blessing. We connected from the first moment. The love that we share and the soul-to-soul connection is authentic, as authentic as if you'd been here all along and grown up with me. Our bond is unbreakable. The Universe sometimes brings to us an expected blessing like this to enhance our lives. The purpose is to share love, experiences, and time, which enriches our soul. You inspire me every day to continue learning and to challenge myself. You have been my teacher, my friend, my blessing, my daughter. You have remained the loving constant in my life that has led me to feel safe with you, experience joy with you, share sorrow with you, and love you deeply, my daughter.

For my beautiful granddaughter, Rose Olivia:

When you lay your head down on your pillow at night, please dream of lollipops and rainbows, and a bouquet of brightly colored roses, my little angel. Dreams do come true when you see them in color. May you always taste the sweetness of lollipops every day of your life, may your life always have the fragrant scent of a rose, and may your life always be filled with the many colors of the rainbow. May all of this lead you to your pot of gold. Know that you are one of the greatest joys of my life, and you have been from the day you were born. I love you to the moon and back.

For my precious little granddaughter, Harper Sydney:

You are my littlest love yet you take up such a huge part of my heart. When I am not with you, I ache to hold you and see that little face smiling at me, and those beautiful eyes staring back at me. On so many levels, you have given me back hope and faith in life, in family, and in love. I have fallen in love with my Harper Sydney, the newest blessing in our family. "I'll love you forever. I'll like you for always. As long as I'm living, my granddaughter you'll be."

Little girls are the most precious gifts—especially daughters, grand-daughters, and nieces. It is our obligation to empower them, teach them, and encourage them to be independent thinkers and doers. We must teach them to explore all that they are curious about. Whatever they may choose to create in their life, whatever they dream of, empower them, teach them, encourage them, and lead by example so that they have a compass, one that will point them in the right direction—their desired direction, wherever that may be spiritually, emotionally, or physically.

Offer them hope and guidance. Plant a seed, watch them evolve, and nurture their efforts. Love them. Applaud them, especially when they are uncertain. Be their soft place to fall and redirect them toward infinite possibilities.

Allow them to grow in their own time and space, and when they seek guidance, do not offer the answer, only suggestions that give them choices, so they can discover the best solution for themselves on their personal journey.

For my heart's inspiration, my son, Matthew:

I am so grateful for the close bond that we have created, and the deep and meaningful conversations that we share. You have faced adversity and challenges with grace, dignity, and integrity, and to say that I am deeply moved by your candor and resilience is an understatement. You continue to inspire me, and your raw music, in which you share your deepest emotions, combined with your incredible and vast musical talent, directly touches that inner knowing that we all experience the same feelings and emotions, and we all sing along to the same song. You have been my biggest cheerleader, and my best friend. Your loving, kind, and compassionate heart is second to none, and with such ease and grace, you have forgiven all that you endured during the active years of my disease. You further connect us all through your poetry and short stories. A universal connection of the soul.

We know that we are always connected. Love knows no space or time. My heart explodes with joy and excitement, topped with great pride in your accomplishments, diligence, hard work, and persistence. You have been creating music for decades and have truly touched so many lives as you deeply connect to the human spirit. You are able to reach into our hearts and draw out our deepest truth, where we say to ourselves, "I am not alone. We are all the same."

You brighten each and every day of my life. Keep moving forward. Keep writing. Keep singing. Keep making music.

You are now embarking upon an exciting new chapter in teaching, traveling, and other cultural experiences to enhance your life. I am so proud of you. When I think about all of the adversity and challenges that you have faced head on, and risen above, I am in awe of your resilience. You are a shining example of perseverance, determination, and discipline, and are requiring more of (and for) yourself so that you can give in excellence to others, and live your best, and most authentic life.

Recently my son said, "You taught me well," "Now I'm thinking like my mom!!" regarding some amazing self-work he has done that has changed the trajectory of his journey, enriching his life. I am so honored and humbled by this sentiment. I'm incredibly proud of my son's dedication and discipline in making the changes he needed to heal and to enhance his life, and practicing commitment and discipline to it all. And sharing it all with me every single step of the way, every day. What a gift. And incredible blessing. This transformation is a mother's gift from her son, which is priceless.

True love embraces every precious part of one's being. Along our journey, we may make mistakes and unintentionally inflict hurt. True love forgives. We have all done the work, individually and collectively. We are family. *Our bonds are cemented in love, and can never be broken.*

Show me your soul, and I'll give you my heart, always and forever.

We practice gratitude for all of the blessings and lessons we are given along our path, which helps us to grow. These detours and "intentional collisions" build strength and endurance so that, when we arrive home, we can stand firmly on a solid foundation in unconditional and unwavering love and commitment. We have the tools to continue to build. These are the tools that we've been practicing with as we have built up, and torn down, made changes, added and subtracted, had successes and life lessons, experienced joy and pain, and felt epiphanies and heartbreak, all the while living our truth. And we are home. Home is where the heart lives … my family. My heart.

My family and my closest friends are my lifeline and my greatest blessings. We all seek connection, compassion, validation, and love. I always feel loved and supported unconditionally.

Who can you count on as part of your support system? How does each one presently show up for you as a loving support on your journey? How do you show up for your loved ones?

_____

_____

_____

_____

_____

_____

Write down what your needs are, and how you would like each one to support you on your journey moving forward. Share it with them.

_____

_____

_____

_____

_____

_____

In what way(s) do you offer love to others?

_____

_____

_____

_____

_____

_____

_____

What does LOVE mean to you?

_____

_____

_____

_____

_____

_____

_____

CHAPTER 15
Daily Reflections and Self-Assessment

Self-reflection is essential for one to continue to evolve. At the end of each day, assess your experiences. Forgive yourself for any *perceived* shortcomings, without any judgement of your actions or thoughts. Begin again with the new day that greets you, and use yesterday's experience to create your desired outcome just for today. There is always another opportunity to choose again tomorrow. It doesn't matter how many mistakes we make; it is about being mindful of the lessons and opportunities we are blessed with which allow us to grow and evolve. How we interpret its meaning is subjective and personal, and we may ask the Universe/God/ Spirit, in prayer and meditation, to assist us in interpreting the meaning of each lesson. Self-awareness, through self-reflection, is a roadmap to our higher selves, where we continuously strive to connect with the Universe, and where we achieve inner peace.

Today's Date is _____ .

My Daily Self-Care Commitment Reminders:

Today:

I will give myself the gift of self-love and self-care. I deserve it!

I will limit my intake of sugar, and other unhealthy foods that are of no nutritional value.

I will engage in "me" time for at least thirty minutes. Choose your personal self-care practices.

I will drink lots of water.

I will get outside for at least thirty minutes and/or exercise.

I will connect with my support system.

I will reach out to one other person to inquire about how they are doing today, because helping others is also a form of self-care.

Add in your own!

1. Today I set an intention to:

(If I begin to feel out of alignment, I will re-center myself by reciting this intention aloud. This reminds me of my daily commitment to my self-care. This re-establishes my position toward my daily goal. I will remind myself that, (for example), "I can choose peace rather than this.")

_____

_____

_____

_____

2. Today I will nourish my soul through the following self-care practice:

_____

_____

_____

_____

3. Today I am grateful for:

_____

_____

_____

_____

4. Today I will let go of one thing that does not serve me which is:

_____

_____

_____

_____

5. In reflection of my day, today I was most proud of:

_____

_____

_____

_____

_____

6. Something I will continue to work on improving at my own pace as an investment in my wellness is:

_____

_____

_____

_____

Note to self: If my noisy thoughts are encouraging me to react in an unhealthy way, I remain in control. I do not react, and I am mindful that I can choose to observe my thoughts without judgement of myself, or others. I will breathe, take a "time out" to practice self-care, and revisit when I feel well. I may also choose to S.P.E.A.R. and S.W.I.M. into Wellness using the steps as outlined in Chapter 6. I will also remind myself to choose the opposite action of what is not serving me.

Some actions/healthy practices of self-care to consider:

- Taking a walk and/or exercising while listening to music that I connect with.

- Coloring an inspirational page to reduce my anxiety.

- Meditation/yoga/prayer/deep breathing with essential oils.

- Cook a healthy meal. Drink water.

- Connect with a friend/family member/professional to talk it through.

- Journal my feelings.

- Volunteer or be of service.

Questions to ask yourself when feeling stressed, anxious, or feeling unwell:

- What will bring me peace/wellness in this situation? In this moment? What action can I take immediately to achieve peace/wellness?

- What do I have absolute control over in this situation? What is this situation trying to show me?

- How does this situation serve my best interest? Or not? How can I honor myself in this situation? Does this situation take into account my own wellness?

- "How do I want to feel today?" What is one self-care practice that I could engage in that would be my action step towards achieving that goal? Do I feel worthy of taking the time to practice my own self-care?

- How will I connect to my spiritual practice to deepen my faith and trust in asking and listening for loving guidance in this situation?

- Who is one person that I trust, with whom I can engage as an accountability buddy? This person has an empathetic ear and will offer me suggestions and guidance as I lead by sharing my goals and intentions. He/she has my best interest at heart, and is willing to be available as my emergency wellness recovery contact 24/7.

- Name and phone number:

7. **Today I feel challenged because:**

_____

_____

_____

_____

My plan of action for my challenge today is:
(choose one simple action step)

_____

_____

_____

8. My short-term goals for this week are: (Choose one or two):

_____

_____

_____

End of Week Self-Assessment:

Week of _____

My strengths were: _____

_____

_____

Things I want to work on: _____

_____

Thoughts/actions/short-term goals for next week based on this week's experiences:

_____

_____

One thought that no longer serves me is _____ ,
and it is a hindrance to my wellness. I am willing to let that go today. If this thought comes back, I will observe the thought, assess if it serves me, and if not, be mindful of choosing the opposite thought/action to achieve a different outcome. I will move at my own pace, and without any self judgment. If it resonates, I will ask God/Spirit/Universe to offer me spiritual solutions and direction.

I will keep moving forward. I am strong. I am in control of my mind. I am grateful for clarity. I am safe. I am aligned with myself, and with the Universe/God/Spirit.

Final Thoughts:

Adapting to my new normal has been a journey in allowing God/Spirit/ Universe aligned with my heart to lead the way as my intuition has guided me to my truth. I unearthed my true desires, passions, and life-calling through focusing on what choices Spirit shares with me that makes my heart open. My vibration is raised by the joy I feel when I am connected to loved ones, to Spirit, my music, exercising, creating in my kitchen, and finding passion in my work—the new normal.

We open the channels of communication that lead and guide us each day to live a life where we discover the energy of our own unique spirits and of our own power. This is where we understand that spirituality is the interconnectedness between ourselves and everything and everyone. We become inspired from within when we listen and when we believe. The guidance is our invitation to connect. We connect and experience our own spirituality in the personal way that we understand and receive God/ Spirit/Universe. This is where our conversations are a deep and meaningful source of a series of small, profound moments, which have the power to push our awareness to a higher level. This creates a transformation of the human spirit.

I will continue on my journey and continue to learn, grow, evolve, and succeed. Yes, I will make mistakes, using each lesson to further evolve and become a better version of myself. I will share my wisdom with others, and look to them for theirs, as we all walk the journey together.

When you know the solution and the path that leads to wellness, to serenity, survival, sanity, self-love, and respect, you want to share it with all those who desire wellness. You have to exercise patience, love, empathy, and acceptance for where one is presently. Hold their hand, reassure them, pray *with* them, and *for* them. Offer them tools and solutions. When someone is unwell, we don't turn our backs on them. We offer them love and support, if they allow it, and help them to find healing remedies and solutions that are sustainable.

We must reassure them that they are safe and encourage them to find the lesson from every feeling and emotion in every situation. We need to remind them over and over that they have the power to heal and grow when they can be open-minded, teachable, humble, and positive, and open to a spiritual practice of their own understanding, rather than living in isolation and in fear.

We must find ways to allow them to see the spectacular human being they inherently are, and that they can evolve to become, and to empower them to accept and embrace change in order to evolve. We must guide them in making good decisions for themselves and in doing the right thing. We must guide them with strength, faith, hope, and love so that they may slowly find their own path and learn to navigate successfully in their lives. Lead by example. Help them to jumpstart a new beginning and then cheer them on from the sidelines. I've always said, from the time I began my recovery, "It takes a village."

Each person has specific needs and goals. Listen, don't preach. Love, don't smother. Guide, don't overwhelm. Meet them where they are. *"Power with," do not "power over."*

Allow them the dignity and respect of being proactive in experiencing wellness. Allow them to explore, and discover in their own time and space, in their own way. If they are unable to participate early on, but they are aware that they need help and ask for it, find resources to help them heal naturally and organically to give the body and the mind a chance to truly heal on a cellular level. Some may need medication. Help them find a medical professional. If they request therapy, help them interview perspective therapists that will be a good fit. Whatever they feel they need, offer to guide them, and always follow up to let them know they are never alone. Remind them that, at any time, they can choose again if their current health and wellness modalities are not serving them.

By being cognizant of the person's mindset and needs, and meeting them where they are, we can help them retrain their thoughts, emotions, and behaviors in wellness, and it validates for them whatever they "know" that they need to heal. Remember, inherently, we all know what we need.

And, we all need validation and support.

Steve once told me at the beginning of my recovery, and of our relationship that he would be my "witness." That gave me heartwarming reassurance that someone who loved me was willing to witness, and validate my journey.

Encouraging self-care and wellness practices promotes a thriving and sustainable recovery. This leads to healthy cells, a healthy immune system, and a healthy body, mind, and spirit.

Healthy foods, mindfulness, meditation, journaling, music, exercise, being of service, positive thoughts, healthy and loving relationships, having fun, good sleep hygiene, a spiritual practice, and daily connection are some of the self-care practices that I use and recommend.

Self-care is the actions that we take to achieve wellness, and wellness is where we stand in our power!

Love and Blessings,
Wendy

Afterword

by
Sheila Pearl

It's often said that in order to move forward in your life, you must take your eyes off the rear-view mirror. When it comes to effective recovery, however, it is important to do *both:* look in the rearview mirror for reference while also watching the road ahead *and* following your GPS.

Funny isn't it, how that GPS can see into the future? "Pot-hole ahead" or "Police ahead" you might hear. It's nice to know what is up ahead before we get there.

The book you have just completed reading is in your rearview mirror, but it is also your GPS, giving you a clear picture of what is ahead of you on your journey, as well as a warning sign of what is ahead of you, which you cannot yet see.

Since Wendy was in her first year of recovery, I have been an integral part of her path toward recovery and her staying on the path each and every day. I have been honored to be witness to the steps she has taken, the lessons she has been learning—and still is learning—as she has been creating a road map for others who are on their journey of recovery. It is not an easy path, nor is it a straight road. As with all success stories, the road to success of any kind is a winding, circuitous route with many detours and redirects. No one achieves success in a vacuum, or without support and guidance.

This is a book to be used as a reference and a reminder over and over again. The tools and exercises Wendy has designed come directly from her own experiences—personal and professional. They are tested and proven effective, because she uses them in her own daily life as well as with her clients and workshop participants.

Using the tools and the example of Wendy's story are the reader's opportunity to apply her road map to moving forward with vision and courage.

What is any "recovery" if not a testimony to the strength and courage of a person's resolve to heal brokenness and pain? With Wendy's roadmap to recovery, one realizes that the pains and challenges of life have created scar tissue, which becomes our connective tissue, which builds our strength and resilience, allowing us to flourish, not simply survive.

Recovery is a form of mastery. When you use Wendy's "GPS" for guidance, you can learn the value of daily practice, application of awareness, and sharing with your support team where you are and what you are experiencing. Your daily practice builds new inner muscle of awareness and the strength to apply new habits of self-nurturing to the ongoing fabric of your tapestry of life.

Sheila Pearl, MSW, CLC
Recalibration Coach and Spiritual Teacher
Author of *The Magic of Big Love: Getting Comfortable with Uncertainty*

Dedications

It is with the deepest gratitude and love that I offer my thanks to so many loving people who took the time, and continue to take the time, to lovingly guide me throughout my wellness journey of recovery from substance use disorder and mental health disorders.

I have been deeply blessed by so many beautiful souls in guiding me, supporting me, and loving me, and so I offer a warm blanket of gratitude to you, and you know who you are. It is because of you that I have evolved, and grown exponentially, and have been blessed to have the daily opportunity to pay it forward. My wellness journey is due in great part to your loving patience and guidance.

I dedicate this book to my loving children: Matthew; Nicole; Olivia; my soul daughter, Sarah; my granddaughter Rose, and my granddaughter, Harper, and my now deceased loving, faithful pup, Max, who was all that I had left at the end, prior to my asking for help to save my life, in addition to my relationship with God. You all saved my life. You are the reason and inspiration behind my successful recovery. It was due solely to the thought of each of you that I had the strength, on April 3, 2013, to ask for help to save my life. I awoke from an overdose after being "out" for two days and realized on this day that, if I took another handful of pills, you would be left without a mother/grandmother, and I couldn't bear the thought of you grieving my death, and never recovering from the loss.

To my beautiful granddaughter, Harper, born on May 19, 2021, you have breathed even more beauty into my life. Just when I thought I had so many blessings already, you made your debut and enhanced my life even more.

I continue to live each day with each of you in my heart, and at the forefront of my mind, and this keeps me present, grateful, determined, disciplined, and dedicated to my recovery, to helping others, and most importantly, to being the mom/grandmother that you deserve. I live each day to offer you all of my love, compassion, support, guidance, and time, at any time that you need it or want it. What I am most grateful for is your forgiveness and understanding of the disease that I lived with for forty years that nearly took my life and affected the dynamic and structure of our family. It is due to your unconditional love and willingness to rebuild our relationships, as well as your respect and all of the times presently that you call me seeking guidance of your own and offering so much love through constant connection, that I am thriving in my recovery. I finally understand what it means to be a mom, and although I am not perfect, I have taken on the role with grace and eagerness to evolve, learning along the journey, and feeling proud of this most important accomplishment. I love you to the moon and back, tooooo much, and always and forever.

To my loving grandparents, Charles and Sylvia Goldman, who were my angels on earth and I know are my guiding angels in Heaven. You are the reason I *am* love. You have instilled in me a deep and profound wealth of love and compassion, which I long to share with others. You are the reason I believe in love. You are the reason I feel loved. You are the reason that I seek to share love, kindness, and empathy. You were a constant living and ever-present example of love. I dedicate this book to you with deep love and gratitude, and in the memory of the profound love, connection, and joy that we shared. Your love continues to sustain me each and every day. I feel your presence with me every day, energetically, through our Spiritual connection.

To my lifelong friends Bill, Vicky, and Joey Kelder. We have lived through it all. You have been a constant loving support for decades, and have been here on my recovery journey, being thoroughly involved and encouraging me since the day I entered the hospital to seek wellness and recovery. You have never given up on me, and have epitomized the true meaning of friendship. Your love and support continue to be a source of strength. You are my family. My ride or die. I love you so much.

To my loving friend Miriam. We are as close as sisters. We have been together as friends for decades, and have watched our children grow up together. You have consistently offered me loving guidance and support throughout our friendship, and most especially throughout my recovery. You "sense" when I need you, and you reach out to offer support. Thank you for being the unpaid "therapist" on call throughout to guide me lovingly back to balance. You have been a constant source of strength. I love you so much.

To my loving friend Marcella Amorese. Thank you for your constant loving support and guidance, and validation of my work in the field of Mental Health Awareness, Wellness, and Education, and your devoted loving friendship. You have been an inspiration, a most brilliant light, and a great source of strength and encouragement in my work and in my recovery.

To my loving friend Gerri Zabusky, aka, my angel. For believing in me and trusting in me, I am forever grateful and humbled. Your loving and selfless nature is an inspiration to so many. I will continue to pay it forward as we "continue to do God's work," as you so eloquently said to me.

To my gorgeous and loving friend Lilyanna Lorelei. Thank you for bringing to life my vision for the cover of this book with such ease and grace, beauty, and deep understanding of my message, and for all of the loving and meaningful conversations that we've shared. We connected immediately, you "got me," heard me, felt me, and brought my vision to life, in living color. I love you dearly.

To my colleague/friend/former Holistic Health Practitioner Lisa D'Alessandro. Thank you for your friendship, sharing your love and wealth of wisdom of holistic healing, for the outstanding care you gave to me in my early my recovery, and for the laughs, walks, talks, and loving friendship. Thank you for inspiring me to become a holistic health practitioner and for all of our collaborations as colleagues.

In honor of my spiritual advisor, loving friend, and inspirational coach/mentor, Sheila Pearl. It is in the darkness that the brightest star shines. Your spark has ignited mine so often, allowing me to find my own way. I see all things clearly now, yet I always look for that little ember constantly glowing softly in the distance, as a reminder that, if the power fails and the darkness returns, you are there to reignite the flame. You have offered loving guidance and support throughout my entire recovery, personally and spiritually. During challenging times, I always knew you were right there beside me, walking with me on my journey. You offered me peace and unconditional love in which I felt comfortable and confident being my authentic self. Thank you for your loving and positive mindset, always leading me to the light.

To my loving friend and former life coach Maria Blon. Thank you for being there to guide me from the beginning. Your loving kindness and guidance at a time of great uncertainty, as I began my recovery, was my deepest source of strength. You were my anchor. You always had faith in me. I am forever humbled by your generosity and loving friendship.

A special note of thanks, with my deepest love and gratitude, go to the following friends/loved ones/earth angels who lovingly guided me in the most difficult of challenges, who never gave up on me, and who encouraged me every step of the way, even when I was unsure of my path. And, to new Spiritual/wellness guides who are offering profound enrichment to my life, and where I am able to pass that on to others.

I am forever grateful, and in awe of your unconditional love, support, and positive impact on my life:

Matthew Friedson, my loving son-in-law

Ranger Friedson, my grand-puppy who always makes me laugh

Deb and Art Friedson, my loving family

Dr. Robert Gregory, for your outstanding initial care, and ongoing in my recovery.

Dr. Bob Gregory, for your outstanding care during the early stages of my recovery.

Amy Prestipino Nichols. With love and gratitude, I thank you for getting me started right out of recovery on a holistic healing path. Your kindness, care and support offered me the chance to begin to truly heal on a cellular level. I am forever grateful to you.

Friends of Recovery-Rockland

James Sexton, Esq., for your willingness to help and support in the early stages of my recovery

Gary Gaber, for your ongoing generosity and patience, working with me tirelessly, and for your support and friendship, with constant reassurance and a smile, even when things seem bleak.

Lija Znakina, for your gorgeous work on my websites, your instant availability and help with my work, keeping me current with my business, and for your sweet friendship, and guidance with Harmonious Health 4 Life, and Write Pray Recover.

Caren Schwartz, who inspires me every day to continue on my journey through her determination and dedication to the cause of raising awareness on substance use disorder and mental health in memory of her beloved son, Reid, who lost his battle with substance use disorder on June 8, 2015. #thisonesforeid

Patti Lemus, for not only being a dear friend but also helping me like a sister would during my active disease, taking me to doctor appointments, taking care of our home when I was unable to, and continuing to be my dear friend today. Your loving friendship has been priceless to me. I hope you know how much I love you and your family.

Mental Health Association of Rockland colleagues who became my second family, and specifically to Stephanie Madison, CEO and President of MHA Rockland, for believing in me and in my recovery, and affording me so many professional opportunities to be trained in the field of mental health and substance use disorder, as well as being a part of so many events that shone a light on mental health, so that I might serve our community fully with experience, knowledge, empathy, and compassion. Stephanie, I am also so grateful for your loving support during the difficult times in my personal life, including the months that my mother was dying. You were a great source of comfort.

Mental Health Association, NYS, for allowing me to be a creator in Mental Health & Wellness 101, for allowing me to speak at various events, for showing such trust in my work and in my recovery, and for always being available to me when I needed specific guidance or had questions. Amy Molloy, Joelle Monaco, thank you for your leadership, guidance, and friendship. As I have told you, you have been mentors to me, willingly and kindly, and I have learned so much from you. I am forever grateful. Thank you.

Keidi Keating. Thank you for your loving guidance and brutal honesty as my editor. When you said to me, "If you want to connect with your readers, you must go back into the manuscript to add in the specific details of your story that will resonate and connect with the public. Everything. The abuse, the trauma, self harm, the episodes of addictive behaviors, everything. I know it will be challenging, but this will be the catalyst in truly helping others." Without that advice Keidi, I never would have had the opportunity to serve others in such a profound way. I greatly appreciate you as an editor, and as my friend.

Friesen Press, specifically Ian and Liza, who were always available and accommodating during the very long process of editing and publishing, and always with a smile. Ian, you are a wonderful publishing specialist. Holding my hand through each process brought great ease and comfort. I truly appreciate all of your guidance and support throughout the process.

Mignyetta Ramnani, for your ongoing validation and support of my recovery from day one, and for trusting in me immediately to serve on your Recovery Unit as a speaker, weekly for eighteen months, in order to serve others living with substance use disorder. You have been a great inspiration to me through the years, as a colleague, friend, and therapist, and have certainly been instrumental in enhancing my recovery. With love and gratitude, I thank you.

Deborah Rooney, for encouraging me from day one in 2013 just because you could. You have empowered me in more ways than you know over the years, and I have always remembered your kindness. Thank you for always thinking of me and always being willing to help. I pay it forward daily. I cherish our friendship dearly.

Dr. Scott Rosa, for your exceptional care—body, mind, and spirit—and for your loving friendship, empathy, and kindness. I always remember not to "catastrophize," and that one piece of advice among so much more that you have blessed me with over the years has been so helpful in enhancing my wellness. You and Jaime Abraham, your loving and kind office manager, were anchors in stormy waters so often, and always with empathy, compassion, patience, and the willingness to help. I am forever grateful.

Scott Berliner, pharmacist, specializing in naturopathy, homeopathy, and functional medicine, for your exceptional care, your invaluable time, your excellent guidance, and friendship as you have guided me throughout my recovery right from the beginning to enhance my wellness using natural and organic solutions as I practice a holistic recovery. I am grateful to you, Jessica, David, Sean, and the rest of your staff who have also taken the time to guide me with patience and kindness throughout my recovery.

Keith and Marissa Jurow, my dear friends who became like family, always willing to help with whatever I needed and always checking in on me, and beautiful, sweet Emma who made me smile each morning. Keith, my brother from another mother, your kindness and compassion gave me great daily comfort and encouragement. Our deep, meaningful conversations, and your brotherly guidance and support, especially early on in my recovery, connects us forever. And in creating my former radio show, The Rx Diaries on Intention Radio, you being my "intro" voice was so awesome and deeply special to me!

Dr. Bruce Levitt, who brought me back to life numerous times, in numerous ways. The most caring and devoted physician I have ever had, and friend, I appreciate you so very much. Thank you for three decades of outstanding medical care, and supporting me unconditionally throughout my recovery. You recently called me a "rockstar" referring to my recovery. Coming from you, that meant the world to me.

To Dr. Arantzazu "Zazu" Cioce PT, DPT, who came into my life at the eleventh hour when I had no idea how to heal my ongoing physical challenges. With a new perspective using an integrative approach, kindness, love, encouragement, excitement, and an eager mindset to assist me in finding within what I needed to heal, in addition to guiding me in physical and mental exercises to enhance my healing, I offer my deepest gratitude. You were an angel sent from Spirit. You have become an integral part of my wellness journey, and a dear, sweet friend. Love you sweetie.

Brett Chinn who came into my life in late 2020, brought together by Spirit. Thank you for your loving Spiritual interpretations and channeling. Your gift has been a blessing to me in moving forward and "cleaning up to make room for my blessings."

Emily Ruaux. My spiritual advisor in business and in my personal life a sacred space. You have channeled such valuable spiritual information and guidance for me always steeped in love and smiles, and always with the greatest of integrity and honesty. Love and light.

Jill Lawrence, my sweet and loving health coach colleague and dear friend. You always make me smile from the inside out, laugh, and think to myself, *I have to hang around more with Jill!* I wish we weren't three thousand miles apart! You are always positive, fun, and willing to help, the most loving fur mama I know, extremely knowledgeable in natural and organic solutions for healing, and is a devoted, loving friend. And my birthday buddy! Love you and am so grateful to have you in my life.

Karen Eastling Ferriello, for your beautiful heart and spirit. You have helped me to move forward when so many times I felt stuck, both personally and professionally. Your loving patience and guidance have seen me through some difficult challenges. Our heartfelt and meaningful conversations have remained so dear to me as direct reminders of God's love and presence throughout my recovery. Your contagious and stunning energy is palpable, and infects my own energy! I love you like my sister.

Deb Studnitzer. Thank you for your never-ending faith in my work and in my recovery, and for your loving friendship. You are so dear to me.

Lynne Warshavsky. Thank you for your loving friendship, and for allowing me to share my ongoing work through my story of recovery within our community. We have become dear friends and kindred Spirits. Your friendship is so dear to me.

Alex McRoberts. The Universe brought us together at the perfect time. You are such a beautiful and loving spirit with your unconditional willingness to guide me, to coach me, both personally and professionally, to teach me, and to offer your friendship with deep compassion and love. We are kindred spirits and sisters of the heart in wellness, and in recovery. Our connection has been life changing and transformative, and has shifted further my entire paradigm of understanding the human condition. I love you my dear friend, and teacher.

In memory of my late mother, Judy Rosen. Thank you for doing your best. I miss you every day. At the end, you told me I was your "inspiration." And although you were not able to find your own strength to follow through my examples of rising above adversity to heal and to continue to live, it still meant the world to me to know how you felt. I know that you tried your best.

I love you.

In overdue memory of my late father, Melvyn Coven. Through my own addictions and mental health disorders, I now understand all of it. I thank you for loving me as best as you could. I know that you watch over me every day. I remember how you used to love to sing (like Sinatra) "My Way." Every time that I hear that song, I know you are with me, and I smile. And there was another song, "Turn Around, Look at Me," by The Vogues, that you would always ask me to sing for you when you visited. Well, Dad, now "turn around; look at me." I am doing okay.

To my sister, Sherry Coven Yeager, always and forever.

As I work each day with those who are living with substance use disorder and mental illness, and as I see first-hand all that they endure, I count myself very blessed to have survived this disease, to be thriving in my recovery, and to have the opportunity to offer others my inspirational story and testimonial of recovery as a light of hope while they themselves navigate their own recovery.

I see myself in every one of the beautiful souls that I work with. I feel the connection, and every day, I am reminded to see each person again as if it were the first time, to look at each one through a refreshed pair of eyes and open perspective. To wonder, "what happened to them," and to try to assist them in healing if they are open.

It's a new day and a new opportunity for change, for growth, and for healing. An opportunity to see each person as myself, to practice great compassion and patience as I would myself, and as I have been treated in my own recovery. It's a chance to pay it forward, to offer love, and to be the change I would like to see in one beautiful soul at a time through the power of love.

Steve once told me to take baby steps as I attempted to take giant leaps. Steve came into my life early on in my journey, and taught me that patience was something I needed to work on, which was—and sometimes still is—daunting, and an ongoing work in progress. He taught me that I need to observe and listen, not to act in an emotional state, as we tend to make impulsive decisions when we do. I continue to practice being non-reactive, listening without judgement, breathing often and just observing my feelings and emotions, to take a timeout, if necessary, and then to respond respectfully, cultivating the most productive and positive outcome for myself and others.

I continue to practice being a good thinker, using the wise mind versus the emotional mind. Steve once said to me, "Like baseball … wait for your pitch." He was saying just observe and listen, and wait for the opportunity to present itself before you respond, calmly, with logic and without emotion." Use the wise mind. The wise mind uses rationale, logic and facts, while the emotional mind responds only based on the emotion that we are feeling.

I am able to apply these principles in my life and in my work with daily repetition, self-awareness, and self-regulation, allowing me to make clear, logical, constructive, creative, and valuable decisions that enhance my life, and the lives of those with whom I surround myself, and those that I serve.

Again, I thank each and every one of you who have been my friend, my coach, my advisor, and my teacher, and for all that have stood beside me, behind me, and loved me unconditionally throughout my recovery.

Love, blessings, and gratitude,
Wendy

About the Author

Wendy Blanchard managed to survive forty years of prescription drug addiction and mental-health disorders before finally enlisting support and help to save her life. Wendy has created necessary change to achieve "whole person wellness" through holistic healthy practices, spiritual solutions and self care. She has created a number of very successful mental-health and wellness literacy development trainings dealing with content such as self-care and wellness practices, spiritual solutions, trauma informed care, and specific tools and strategies in adapting a wellness mindset. These tools and strategies are sustainable and offer the opportunity to thrive in recovery.

Wendy has very recently, in October, 2021, created and launched "Whole Person Wellness: An Integrative Approach to Recovery" which is an interactive workshop series using an integrative approach to recovery body, mind and spirit through mindfulness techniques and expressive writing. It has met with outstanding reviews.

Wendy holds certifications from the National Council for Behavioral Health (Mental Health First Aid for Youth and Adults), the NYS Suicide Prevention Center (Suicide Safety for School Staff), and the NY Peer Specialist Certification Board (Certified Peer Specialist), and is an Integrative Nutrition Holistic Health Coach and consultant with a private practice, working with clients in recovery from mental illness and substance use disorder. She can also be accessed as a "Verified Practitioner" through www.myhelpconnect.com which is a collaborative community of providers working together to serve those living with mental health disorders. Also in October, 2021, Wendy has begun a campaign for a "culture and climate shift" for global wellness. She is offering her workshops, and hosting social media LIVE event discussions to bring much needed awareness to mental health/substance use disorder. She is sharing the components of her "Integrative Approach to Recovery" program through her social media platforms. She is also inviting others living in recovery to join her in these LIVE discussions to share their stories and experiences to further serve the global community. Wendy stands firmly in her faith that with her groundbreaking program of a wellness approach to recovery using her methods of an integrative approach through the body, mind and spirit, guided by God/Spirit/Universe, we can create a ripple effect globally. Wendy believes that we can create global wellness through awareness, education about integrative practices to achieve wellness, and through having an ongoing dialogue to normalize mental health.

Wendy also works with school districts, libraries, frontline workers, mental health professionals, and NY State Friends of Recovery, as well as local chapters of Friends of Recovery to provide trainings that will empower communities in an understanding of mental health, and Substance Use Disorder, changing the language, and supporting all of us in a public health approach. "We all have mental health."

The recipient of the "Worldwide Who's Who" award in 2013, as Professional of the Year, for her blog "The Rx Diaries" (no longer "live"), Wendy's story also appears in the 2015 book Living Passionately: *21 People Who Found Their Purpose – and How You Can Too!*

Wendy currently lives in Orange County, NY, surrounded by her loving children—Matthew, Nicole, and Olivia, her soul daughter, Sarah, her grandchildren, Rose and Harper, and her extended family, and close friends.

CPSIA information can be obtained
at www.ICGtesting.com
Printed in the USA
BVHW071955300122
627572BV00005B/184